Sketches of the city of Detroit : state of Michigan, past and present, 1855.

Robert Ellis Roberts

SKETCHES

OF THE

CITY OF DETROIT,

STATE OF MICHIGAN,

PAST AND PRESENT.

1855.

DETROIT.
R. F. JOHNSTONE & CO., PRINTERS, ADVERTISER OFFICE.
1855.

Entered according to an Act of Congress in the Clerk's Office of the District Court of the United States for the District of Michigan, by Robert E. Roberts

Sketches of the City of Detroit.

The following brief sketches of the history, pecuniary condition, resources and prospects of the city of Detroit, compiled from authentic data, will in part supply information frequently sought after.

THE CITY—ITS HISTORY

The city of Detroit is situated on the north shore of the Detroit river or strait connecting Lakes Erie and St. Clair. The river is the boundary line between Michigan and Canada West. The city is 18 miles east of Lake Erie, and 7 miles west of Lake St. Clair, 300 miles west of Buffalo, and 515 from Washington, in Latitude 42 degrees 19 minutes 53 seconds north, and Longitude West 82 deg. 58 sec. or from Washington west 5 deg. 56 min. 12 sec. Difference in time from Washington 33 min. 44 sec. New York city 34 min. 48 sec.

The history of Detroit is most intimately connected with the history of the whole north-west, as its settlement dates among the first on the American continent. Founded in the strife for sovereignty between the English and French governments, it became at an early day a point of central influence, importance and action. No place in the United States, it has been observed, presents such a series of events, interesting in themselves, and permanently affecting as they occurred, its progress and prosperity. Five times its flag has been changed. First the lily of France floated over its fortress, then the red cross of England, and next the stripes and stars of the United States, and then again the red cross, and lastly the stripes and and stars.

Three different sovereigns have claimed its allegiance, and since it has been held by the United States its government has been thrice transferred; twice it has been besieged by the Indians; once captured in war, and once burnt to the ground. Fire has scathed it—the tomahawk, scalping knife, and war club have been let loose upon it in the hands of an unrelenting savage foe. It has been the scene of one surrender, of more than fifty pitched battles, and twelve horrid massacres.

The present site of the city was occupied by Indian villages at the period of the discovery of the country. In 1610 it was first visited by the French. The whole lake region from its discovery until 1762 was under the dominion of France. The legitimate settlement of the city was in 1701, at which time a fort called "Ponchartrain" was erected. Its location was south of Jefferson Avenue and east of Shelby street, occupying a space of about 200 feet square, and recently while some workmen were excavating for the foundation to the improvements now being made to, and in rear of the Michigan Exchange, they came across some of the cedar pickets of the palisades which encircled the fort. In 1749 emigrants were sent here from France at the expense of the government. Here in 1763 that daring warrior Pontiac the great head of the Indian race at that period, entered upon a bold plan of driving every white man over the Alleghanies and destroying all the English posts in the north west, simultaneously on a fixed day. These consisted of thirteen well garrisoned forts, stretching from Niagara and Pittsburgh all along the lakes to the Mississippi, and on the Wabash river. So secret were his plans, and so prompt was he in their execution, that ten of these forts fell in a single day, and their inmates were massacred—but he himself met with a signal defeat at Detroit. During that year it was ceded to the British crown. In 1778 Fort Shelby was erected by the British commandant Major Le Noult, and called Fort Le Noult until after the war of 1812, when it was named in honor of Governor Shelby of Kentucky. It was located at the intersection of Fort and Shelby streets, and was removed in 1827. In 1796, Captain Porter with a detachment of the American Army, under Gen. Wayne, entered the city and took possession of the fort, which had been previously evacuated by the British, and hoisted the first flag bearing the stripes and stars that ever floated in the Wolverine State.

The ordinance of 1787 was then extended over this part of the north west territory which was governed by its first magistrate Gen. Arthur St. Clair.

The first Lodge of Free and Accepted Masons in Detroit was organized at the house of James Donaldson under sanction of the Grand Lodge of Canada, Dec. 19th, 1794, which was styled "Zion Lodge No. 10." James Donaldson was the first W. M.

The Territory of Michigan was formed in 1805, and William Hull was appointed the first Governor, with a judiciary, composed of Augustus B. Woodward, James Griffin and Francis Bates, Judges, who organized a government at Detroit in July of that year. On the 11th of June previous, the town was almost entirely destroyed by fire, one house only remaining. Shortly after the catastrophe an act of Congress was passed directing the governor and judges to lay out a new town including the site of the one destroyed and ten thousand acres of adjacent land.

In 1807 Judge Bates resigned and James Witherall was appointed in his place.

In 1809 Rev. Gabriel Richard, published the first newspaper printed in the city, styled the "Michigan Essay or Imperial Observer." James M. Miller, printer.

January 19, 1811. At a meeting of the Governor and Judges, Augustus B. Woodward, one of the Judges, himself clothed, completely in American manufactures, moved the following resolution.

"Whereas, the encouragement of American manufactures is a duty imposed on the good citizens of the United States, by the dictates of benevolence as well as by the injunctions of patriotism, and whereas the consumption of domestic manufactures is at the same time the most simple and most efficacious encouragement of them, and whereas it is at all times becoming that those who receive both honors and emoluments from the execution of public trusts, should exhibit themselves the foremost in examples of utility, therefore, Resolved, that it be respectfully and earnestly recommended by the Legislative authority of the Territory of Michigan, to all officers of this government, to appear clothed in articles the manufacture of the continent of North America at all times when engaged in the execution of any public duty, power or trust from and after the fourth day of July, 1813."

Which was passed unanimously, and a copy thereof signed by the members and attested by the Secretary in order that it be deposited in the office of the Secretary of the Territory. And the Secretary to take such measures for the further publication and communication of the same as he may judge expedient."

January 1812. At a meeting of the Governor and Judges, a committee to whom was referred a communication from the commissioners of internal navigation in the State of New York reported as follows:

"Whereas, the commissioners of internal navigation in the State of New York, have addressed to the Governor and Judges of the Territory of Michigan, a communication, relative to a canal in the State of New York which being considered, Resolved unanimously, that in the opinion of the undersigned the canal contemplated by the commissioners of internal navigation in the State of New York from Black Rock to Rome, would not be so desirable as a canal around the cataract of Niagara, another by the falls of the Oswego." The report was adopted and at a subsequent meeting the Governor and Judges signed a letter addressed to Gov Morris, Dewitt Clinton, William North, Thomas Eddy, Robert R Livingston and Robert Fulton Esquires, commissioners of internal navigation of the State of New York, enclosing a copy of the above resolution.

Reuben Atwater, acting Governor, A. B. Woodward and James Witherell, Judges, composed the meeting.

Here that brave and magnanimous chief Tecumseh, the noblest of his race, "rose, reigned and fell." Tecumseh participated against us in all the conflicts, from the defeat of Harmar in 1790, to the battle of the Thames in 1813, where he lost his life, and left no spot or blemish on his honor or humanity.

On the 16th of August, 1812, Detroit fell into the hands of the British. It was retaken by the American army in 1813, and the territorial government re-organized in the fall of that year, by the appointment of Gen Lewis Cass, as Governor, who immediately took up his residence at Detroit, which has ever since been his home.

The President of the United States, James Monroe, visited Detroit in the month of August, 1817. His arrival was celebrated by the firing of cannon, a public dinner and a grand illumination of the city at night. He was on an excursion for personal observation, of the country, having passed through the New England states and visited various important points along the St. Lawrence, Lake Ontario, and Niagara river, to Buffalo, where he embarked for this city in a sail vessel, and visited various points upon Lake Erie. The citizens of Detroit presented him with a span of horses and carriage, with which he returned to Washington by land, visiting all important points in Ohio, Pennsylvania and Maryland. Mr Monroe was the only President of the United States who ever visited Detroit, during his official term.

In 1817 John P. Sheldon published a newspaper styled the "Detroit Gazette," which was the first successful newspaper printed in Michigan.

With every natural facility of becoming a place of importance, the condition of Detroit for many years depended on the precarious support afforded by the fur trade, the disbursement of public moneys while a military post, and the liberal appropriations by government for public objects.

The impulse and effect produced by the settlement and cultivation of the surrounding country was wanting until about the year 1830, when emigration, which had previously been small, rapidly increased, and farms and small villages began to thicken along the lines of the turnpike roads which had been constructed by the general government. These were the Chicago, leading to Illinois the Saginaw, to the head of Saginaw Bay, the Fort Gratiot to the foot of Lake Huron, and the Grand River to Lake Michigan at the mouth of Grand River

DETROIT IN 1778—Interesting Narrative.

The compiler is indebted to Hon Alexander D Fraser, for the following very interesting sketch.

The following narrative was taken down from the lips of James May, Esq , my father-in-law, who died in January, 1829. He was an Englishman who came to this place when a young man, in 1778. He was Chief Justice of Common Pleas, established here immediately after General Wayne took possession of the country, under Jay's treaty, was Colonel of Militia, &c. When the American Flag was hauled down by order of Genl. Hull, in 1812, at the time of the surrender, he got possession of it, and kept it until Genl Harrison arrived, when it was again hoisted. A D F

My Note Book, 1826

In the year 1778, after a passage of four days from Fort Erie, I arrived by the brig-of-war Genl. Gage, at the settlement of Detroit. No vessels at that time navigated upon the lakes, upon account of the revolutionary war which then raged, excepting those of His Majesty— not even the smallest craft had this permission. Previous to that time, but few vessels ever visited the lakes, and those very few and of an inferior class—indeed, no merchant vessel had as yet ploughed the waves of the lakes.

The old town of Detroit comprised within its limits that space between Mr. Palmer's store (Conant Block) and Capt. Perkins' house, (near the Arsenal building,) and extended back as far as the public barn, and in front was bordered by the Detroit river. It was an oblong square, and covered about two acres in length, and an acre and a half in breadth. It was surrounded with oak and cedar pickets about fifteen feet long. The town had four gates, east, west, north and south. Over the first three of these gates were block houses. Each of these had four guns, (six-pounders, each.) The first of these was in that space intervening between Palmer's shop, and Judge Door's house, (opposite Ives bank.) The west block-house was before the ground on which Capt. Perkins' house now stands. The third block house was at the north gate, which was inside of a small bridge that is on the road to the fort, and near the public magazine, (Mr. Austin's house, Congress street.) There were besides two six gun batteries fronting the river, and in a parallel direction with the block houses. There were four streets that run east and west; the main street was twenty feet wide and the rest fifteen feet wide. There were three cross streets, running north and south, from ten to fifteen feet wide. At that time there was no fort, but there was a citadel on the ground on which Perkins' house now stands, (N. W. corner of Jefferson avenue and Wayne street,) the pump of which still remains there. The citadel was picketed in, and within it were erected barracks of wood, two stories high, sufficient to contain ten offices; and there were barracks sufficient to contain from three to four hundred men; a provision store built of brick. There was also within the citadel an hospital and guard house.

In the town of Detroit, in the year 1778, there were about sixty houses, most of them of one story high, and a few of them a story and a half, but none of them were two stories. They were all of logs, some hewn and some round. There was also a building of a splendid appearance, called the King's Palace. It was two stories high. It was situated near the east gate, and stood where Conant's new building (Beecher's store) now stands. The pump which now stands behind that building stood in the rear of the Government House. Attached to this house was a large garden extending towards the river, which contained many fruit trees. When I came here it was occupied by Governor Hamilton, for whom it was built. He was the first Governor commissioned here by the British Government, and was here about three years before I came. There were four companies of the Eighth Regiment, two companies of Butler's Rangers, and one company of the Fourth Regiment. The latter were under the command of Capt. Anbey, the former under Capt. Caldwell, and Eighth Regiment commanded by Major Leverault, who was also commanding officer of the post and its dependencies. All these constituted about 500 troops. There was a guard-house near the west gate, and another near the Government House. Each of these guards consisted of twenty-four, and a subaltern officer, who mounted regularly every morning between nine and ten o'clock. Each of these guards furnished four sentinels who relieved every two hours. There was also an officer of the day who did strict duty. All these gates were shut regularly at sun-set, and even wicket gates were shut at 9 o'clock regularly, and the keys were delivered into the hands of the commanding officer. They were opened in the morning at sunrise. No Indian whatever, or squaw was permitted to enter the town with any instrument, such as a tomahawk, or even knife. It was a standing order that the Indians should deliver these before they were permitted to pass, into the hands of the sentinel, and they were restored when he returned. No more than twenty-five Indians were allowed to come into town at the same time—they were permitted to come in only at the east and west gates. At sun-set the drum beat, and all the Indians were compelled to leave town instantly. It was always the signal; strict search was made by the soldiers that none might be concealed; and if it was discovered that even a squaw was secreted but for a night, severe reprehension was sure to follow.

There was a Council House, for the purpose of holding council with the Indians. It was near the water side, rear of the Government House. There was a Roman Catholic Church situated where Payne's brick house now stands, (near the Masonic Hall.) The Priest was then Peter Simple, an aged and infirm man, and adjoining it was the Priest's house and burying ground. The church was 60 by 40 feet, one story high, with two steeples and two bells.

The population of the town was sixty families, in all about two hundred males and one hundred females. They—the men—were chiefly bachelors. There was not a marriage in the place for a number of years, until I broke the ice. Twenty of these persons were traders and kept retail stores. Of the population there were 30 Scotchmen, 4 Englishmen and 15 Irishmen.

The extent of the settlement up the Detroit River, reached about Hudson's House (now Fisher's) not a house above that place in this country, until you reached Michilimackinac, where there was a small settlement. Below Detroit it was settled on the banks of the River as far as Springwells, but not beyond that. These settlements were entirely confined to the bank of the River, and there was no settlement or improvement in any other part of this Territory than that in the immediate vicinity of Detroit. These settlers were all French Canadians, and the whole population of the settlement, exclusive of the Military, might be about 700 souls. It was at that time considered a journey to go from Springwells into the other extremity of the settlement.

The Indian trade was then excellent. There was much public money then in circulation here, for the troops and the Navy Department, were then strong here. This post was established by the British to keep the Indians in check, of whom they were afraid, and this was the reason why the old town was built so compact, that it might in case of urgency be more able to defend it against the assaults of the Indians. The different tribes were Hurons, Wyandotts, Chippewas and Pottawattamies, Taweys and the Moravians. Frequently between 3 and 500 of these could be seen at a time during the revolutionary war. The civil department consisted of two Justices of the Peace, one of these was the late Thomas Williams Esq, (father of the late Maj Gen. John R. Williams) and the other was the Governor or Commanding officer, for the time. The Orderly Sergeant was the Constable. The justice kept the peace, and the commanding officer took cognizance of all cases under £10 York. For all sums above this, writs came from Montreal, addressed to Williams, who got his Bailiff to execute them.— In case of small debts, on a complaint to the Commanding officer, he sent his orderly to the debtor, requesting his immediate attendance before that officer. He would then hear the parties and make his determination accordingly. If against the defendant, he would order him instantly to pay the money, or send him to the Guard House until he complied, and some times would give a little time to pay, there was no process or costs in these cases. If the debtor, however, had no property, the party was set at liberty. One Granchin owed me a debt. I complained to Gov Hamilton, who sent for him. He came, and being asked if he had any thing to say against the debt, he said no. He then ordered him to give me an old negro wench in payment, and she served me twenty-five years.

1779.—The Governor, getting tired of administering Justice, proposed to the merchants to establish a Court of Trustees with jurisdiction extending to ten pounds Halifax. Eighteen of these Trustees entered into a Bond that three of them should be a weekly Court in rotation, and that they should defend any appeal which might be taken to the Courts of Montreal. This court lasted for about eighteen months, and none ever appealed from it. It was considered as a court of conscience. They had certain forms of process,—they rendered judgment, and issued executions. They had a constable and a Clerk, and imprisoned their prisoners in the Guard House.

Our goods were imported from Montreal. The only mode of conveyance was by the King's ship, who delivered them here free of freight.

When an Indian committed a depredation on the Canadians they generally rose in a body, and hung the Indian without any ceremony. The citizens depended principally for eatables on the Indians who supplied them with the quadrupeds of the forest. A milch cow was then generally sold for one hundred dollars, and a pair of steers would sell for two hundred and fifty dollars.

The circulating medium in the country consisted chiefly of paper money issued by the merchants, from a sixpence to twenty shillings, and purported to be payable to the bearer. Permission was given by the Governor to strike off so much money in shin plasters as a person had property to redeem in that month. The property was valued by appraisers, or a bond was given with security to redeem. On the day of payment, each trader exchanged with him who had his bills, and this was found to answer every purpose of trade, and seldom or ever any loss accrued from this mode of dealing. At this time the Indians used to spear the fish, and sell them here for rum and whiskey.

The citizens all lived then like one family,—had Detroit assemblies where ladies never went without being in their silks. The people dressed very richly. Assemblies were once a week, and sometimes once a fortnight. Dining parties were frequent, and they drank their wine freely.

DETROIT IN 1805. Before the Fire.

The old town previous to the fire, occupied a site embraced within the following limits: Griswold st. on the east, and Cass street on the west, and extending from the river to Larned street, secured by a stockade on the west and east running from the river to Fort Shelby (present north line of Congress street.) In rear of the fort was the Royal Military garden, on the east the Commanding Officers Field, and east of the stockade on the bank of the river was the Navy Garden. Where Woodward avenue now is, and between Woodbridge and Atwater streets was the Navy Yard. The names of the streets in the old town were St. Louis, St. Ann, St. Joseph, St. James, St. Honore and L'Erneau. The width of the widest (St. Ann) was but 20 feet, at either end of which were gates forming the only entrances into the city. A carriage way which was called *Chemin du Ronde*, encircled the town just inside the palisades. A large creek called 'River Savoyard' bordered by low marshy grounds separated the high ridge upon which the old town was built, from the high grounds along the summit of which runs at present Fort street. This creek extended from the river near the lower line of the Cass farm, along a line between Congress and Larned streets to Woodward avenue, and across Congress street and Michigan avenue, into Fort street, thence east along the line of Fort street. That part of the town not required for public use was subdivided into 59 lots. The names of freeholders in the old town were Askin, Abbott, McDonald, McDougall, Meldrum, Parke, Grant, Chagrin, McGregor, Campau, McKee, Oadney, Macomb, Roe, Howard, Tremble, Sparkin, Leith, Williams, Ridley, Frazer, Haines, Dolson, Jayer, Lefoy, Thebauld, Duhamel, St. Cosmo, Belanger, LaFleur, Cote, Scott, LaFontaine, Bird, Starling, Andrews, Harsoy and Ford.

The destruction of the old town was so far fortunate that it led to the adoption of a plan better adapted to a city, such as Detroit has become.

THE NEW TOWN.

The site of the city is an elevation of about 30 feet, along the river front, rising farther back to about 60 feet, affording most perfect drainage, covering an area within its corporate limits of 3368 acres, about one-third of which is closely covered by buildings. These limits will probably be enlarged on the river front in each direction at the meeting of the next Legislature.

The Governor and Judges who laid out the new town, seemed to anticipate the future importance of the city, and to their foresight, good taste and judgment, are we indebted for the reserves of the Grand Circus, Campus Martius, East, West, Centre and Capitol Parks, and the numerous wide avenues, from 120 to 200 feet in width.

It is in contemplation now to soon embellish the parks and circuses with public fountains.

Detroit was incorporated a city by an act of the Governor and Judges in 1815, seven years before Boston bore the name and privileges of a city, and the government was vested in five trustees. This act was suspended in 1824, by a new charter passed by the Legislative council, when the late Gen. John R. Williams, was chosen Mayor.

Sec. 1, of the act of 1815 reads as follows:

"Be it enacted, by the Governor and Judges of Michigan that so much of an 'Act to repeal all Acts of the parliament of England and of the parliament of Great Britain within the Territory of Michigan in the United States of America, and for other purposes" as repeals "An Act to incorporate the Town of Detroit " enacted by the Legislative Council and House of Representatives of the North Western Territory, in General Assembly, approved at Chillicothe on the eighteenth day of January in the year of our Lord one thousand eight hundred and two, be and the same are hereby repealed." Hon. Solomon Sibley, was chairman of the first Board of Trustees, and Thomas Rowland, Secretary. In 1816 the Board consisted of George McDougall, Abram Edwards, Oliver W. Miller, Peter J. Desnoyers and Stephen Mack. George McDougall chairman, and Thos. Rowland, Secretary.

The first public market house was erected in 1816 by Capt. Benj. Woodworth, under a contract with the Trustees, at a cost of fifteen hundred dollars. It was built in the centre of Woodward avenue, a little south of Jefferson avenue, and covered a space of about 30 by 70 feet, one story high, composed merely of a roof supported by posts, and enclosed with slats three inches apart, and served as a public whipping place until the law was repealed. The culprits were placed outside with their hands thrust through the slats and tied on the inside, when the officer would apply the lash on the bare back of the victim.

When Detroit was first incorporated as a city, the only road leading out of it was the one up and down the river. The mail was brought around the lake, through Ohio, on horseback, and when the road was very bad a man carried it on his shoulders through the Black Swamp. The first line of carriages between Detroit and Ohio was established in 1827.

Detroit is a port of entry, the commercial metropolis of the State of Michigan, and occupies a central position on the great chain of rivers and lakes two thousand miles in extent, and forming together the greatest body of inland navigable waters in the world.

The following will show in a condensed form, estimates of the mean, length, breadth, depth, area and elevation of the several bodies of water which compose the great chain.

	LENGTH MILES	BREADTH MILES	DEPTH FEET	ELEVATION FEET	AREA IN SQUARE MILES
Lake Superior	400	80	900	187	32,000
Green Bay	100	20	500	56	2,000
Lake Michigan	3.0	70	1000	578	22,400
Lake Huron	240	60	1000	574	20,400
Lake St. Clair	20	18	20	570	360
Lake Erie	240	40	84	565	9,600
Lake Ontario	180	35	500	232	6,300
River St. Lawrence			20		940
					91,000

The location of the city is pleasant, commanding a fine view of the surrounding country, with Canada in the foreground, and of the river for miles above and below until intercepted by beautiful islands. It was originally selected by the *natives* of the forest with their usual sagacity, as a site for their villages, and was thus occupied before the Lake Country was discovered by Europeans two hundred and forty-five years ago, and for about ninety years afterwards, or until the year of our Lord 1701, when it was taken possession of by the French who erected "Fort Ponchartrain" for the purpose of establishing a fur trading post, and protecting the traders.

TIME'S CHANGES.

The compiler of these sketches first visited this city in the spring of 1827, without any intention of permanently locating here, but a short residence sufficed to render his attachment enduring, and it has ever since been his home. Having never been from it more than a few weeks at a time, visiting eastern cities, and at each successive return he has hailed with delight his approach to the good old City of the Straits, up its beautiful river of the purest of water. There is no other *de troit* like it, with its elevated shores, lined with villages, villas, stately mansions, French farm-houses, windmills, and pear trees of more than a century's growth, its broad stream deep and clear with no *veto* "sandbars" or "snake-heads" to *interrupt*, and no fleet of "Steam Tugs" and "Lighters" to *aid* navigation.

Detroit in 1827 was the only municipal corporation in the territory of Michigan. It contained a population at that time of about two thousand souls, which was about one-tenth the population of the whole territory, who were settled along the Lakes and rivers, from Monroe to St. Clair, Mackinaw and Green Bay, and but little was known of the interior of the territory, which was for the most part a wilderness of forest and prairie, though a few scattered settlements had been made in Washtenaw and Oakland counties, with here and there a log-house. A water flour mill had been erected a year or two previous at Pontiac, by Col. Stephen Mack and Hon. Solomon Sibley, which was the first in Michigan.

The city at that time was but little else than a military and fur-trading post. The inhabitants were principally native French, though there were a number of families here from the eastern States, but not more than a dozen from any foreign country.

The buildings were mostly constructed of wood, one or two stories high, with steep roofs and dormer windows. The banks of the river within view of the city were studded with wind grist mills, and flour was brought to the city and sold only in sacks. Since that time great changes have taken place, and scarcely a vestage of the old city remains. A great portion of the then limits of the city, have been swept over by fire and re-built with substantial business buildings.

Then the steam boat arrivals were three or four a week, now there are eight or ten a day.

Then there were but three or four wharves at which vessels could unlade, now its docks extend for more than two miles. Then there were but two or three turnpike roads leading from the city, now there are plank roads and railroads in every direction.

Then a mail from the east arrived once or twice a week, now we have three or four from the east daily, and the telegraph wires extending in various directions, permitting instant communication with far distant points.

(The telegraph line was completed to Detroit, and dispatches were received from the city of New York for the first time, March 1st, 1848.)

Then the fronts of the residences of James Abbott, Col. Anderson, Gen. Larned, the brothers Cote, Mrs. Deveraux and Dr. Hurd, situated on the west side of Woodward avenue, between the river and Congress street, were shaded by an almost continuous row of stately trees. There was the old meat market in Woodward avenue, below Jefferson, and the old wooden Presbyterian church, corner of Larned street and Woodward avenue. The residence of Robert Smart, Esq., south of the Church, and at the corner of Woodward avenue and Woodbridge street was the Godfrey House, nearly opposite was Smith's Tavern. Where the "National" now stands, there was a small yellow house in the centre of a large potato lot, and beyond was a vast common, the Jail, where Centre Park now is, the Methodist Church a little to the east, Cliff's Tavern near the grand circus, Gen. Williams barn, and an occasional shantee. These were all that intercepted a view of the forest beyond.

In Judge Sibley's field, west of Woodward avenue and north of the residence of Dr. Duffield, was a small Fort, called Fort Croghan, which had been thrown up by the citizens and mounted with a few pieces of artillery for the purpose of protecting the inhabitants against the incursions of the Indians, who came from the woods and drove off cattle that were feeding on the commons and murdered the inhabitants.

On Jefferson avenue, west of Woodward, there were in the first two blocks a number of small stores—interspersed with dwellings, and those extended to the line of the Cass farm just below Cass street

The "Cass Farm" was then a farm with but the farm house, barns, &c, and an Indian store house and distillery on the lower line, and an ox mill on the river front

The first block in Jefferson Ave east of Woodward was occupied on either side by small stores, and on the N W corner of Bates street was the store and dwelling of Peter J Desnoyer, Esq. On the south east corner the store and dwelling of Gen J R Williams, east of which was Pat Palmer's tavern, and the residences of John Whipple Judge Chipman and Barnabus Campau Esq, and on the corner the Masonic Hall and Council House. Crossing Randolph street on the site now occupied by the "Biddle House" was the brick residence of Maj John Biddle—constructed by Governor Hull, in 1807, and it was the first brick house built in the city, and next the residence of Hon E A Brush, opposite was the brick residence and extensive fruit garden of Judge Sibley. On the north west corner of Randolph street was the Bank of Michigan, formerly occupied by the Detroit Bank, chartered in 1806 and broke in 1810 and west were the residences of Major Kearsley, Dr Brown and Thos F Knapp. All these are now gone, and with the exception of the old arsenal and the residence of the late P S Wordell, Jos Campau's dwelling, and Smart and Desnoyer's stores not a building remains along the whole extent of Jefferson avenue which was existing in 1827.

Jefferson avenue until about this time terminated at the line of the Brush farm, when it was opened up as far as Russell street but with stern opposition from the owners of the farms. There were then no buildings to obstruct the view of the fields and woods beyond, from the avenue in the vicinity of Brush street. The only road at the time to Hamtramck and Gross Point was on the river beach to gain which from the avenue down Randolph street you passed the Steamboat Hotel, the principal tavern in the city kept by Capt Benj Woodworth brother of the author of the "Old Oaken Bucket". Capt W emigrated to this city in 1806, and now resides at St Clair. Nearly opposite the hotel was the residence of Dr McCoskrey, uncle of the present worthy Episcopal Bishop of the diocese of Michigan. Doct McC came to Detroit with Wayne's army in 1796, of which he was the surgeon. Turning from Randolph into Atwater st on the south was the Carding and Full Cloth Factory of Messrs French & Eldred, and just beyond, at the foot of Brush street was the Smith Shop of Harvey Williams in front of which Che-minck, son of that notorious Indian Chief, Kish-ka-go killed an Indian. Kish-ka-go and son were arrested and lodged in Jail. Kish-ka-go supposed that he was detained for the murder of some white man, he having killed several and he could not be persuaded to the contrary, though informed of the fact by Col Beaufait. His reply to the Col was, "no the hats never forget." Kish-ka-go called himself the "son of thunder." He sent a messenger to Saginaw with instructions to summons his band together and hold a wa-bi-no to importune thunder, (his father) to come and throw down the jail and liberate him, on a particular day he named. The Chief waited patiently and sullenly for the day when he was to be liberated. The day came, but thunder did not, and he committed suicide by taking poison furnished by his squaw. Che-minck, escaped from the Jail and was not retaken.

East of Randolph street, extending along the front of the Brush, Beaubien, Moran, Rivard, Mullet, Gouin and Dequindre Farms were extensive old Pear Orchards of centurial trees—they having been transplanted there from that enchanted garden of Europe—"La belle France"—by the early French imigrants who brought the young trees with them. In front of these was a green lawn with a gentle slope to the beach of the river

Annually, in the month of June, thousands of Indians came from the Upper Lakes on their way to Malden to receive presents from the British Government, who stopped and lined the beach with their birchen canoes, and pitched their tents beneath the shade of these trees,

12 SKETCHES OF THE CITY OF DETROIT.

On recalling to memory those old Pear trees, and the green lawn beneath and in front of them, the many pleasant hours spent rambling there, eating of their delicious fruit, we contemplate with regret the changes—scarce half a dozen of the old trees remaining, the iron rails are stretched, and the fizing and rumbling of the iron horse is heard where they were. On turning down the river to the other line of the city, and recalling the delightful promenade along the high banks of the river, which at this point formed a beautiful bay, across the fronts of the Cass, Jones, Forsyth, LaBrosse, Baker and Woodbridge farms and sweeping down past the residences of Robert Abbott, and Judge May, and reflecting that this too, has been sacrificed and leveled low, to accommodate commercial and railway facilities, still more does it cause one to regret that the Star of Empire in its westward flight visited the City of the Straits. It makes one almost sigh with the ancient *habitans* at the remembrance of those times when the city was visited by an occasional steamer to bear away the furs, fish and sugar brought hither in the birch canoe, from the lake country above, and wish for the return of the good old days when the Indian canoe, French callash, carryall and charrette were the only vehicles of conveyance. But few of the buildings of that day now remain. The most compact part of the city was between Jefferson avenue and the river, and the only buildings of that day now standing there, are Jos. Campau's dwelling on Jefferson avenue, and the Hanks house on Bates street; all the rest are gone, and the most of them were swept off by fire.

On Woodward avenue the dwelling of John Owen Esq. now occupied by John Webster is a hardware store is the only one remaining. Besides these, there is the old farm house of Gen. Cass, which is now on the north side of Larned street. The brick dwellings of Messrs. Jackson and Cooper, on Michigan avenue, the Academy near the water works office on Bates street, the Browning House farther up, the Cathedral of St. Ann, and part of the Bishops palace since encircled by brick, the Abbott house opposite, (which was on that spot when the town was destroyed by fire in 1805 and it is the only one of that day, except the Moran farm house on Woodbridge street, now remaining in the limits of the city.) The Andre house on Randolph street, and the one opposite occupied by the Catholic sisters' School and the dwelling of Mr. McDonald, corner of Fort and Shelby sts., formerly the quarters of the commanding officers of Fort Shelby.

The above it is believed, are the only buildings of 1827 that now remain, except some that may have been re-built or re-modeled so as not to be identified at this time.

Fort Shelby was removed in 1827—8, and the earth was used in filling up the embankment then being constructed along the whole water front of the city, by order of the authorities, the expense of which was assessed on the adjoining property. This was done as a sanitary measure, and the health of the city, which a year or two previous had been bad, was very much improved.

MAYORS.

The following gentlemen have held the office of Chief Magistrate of the city, and were elected as follows:

John R. Williams, elected in 1824; John R. Williams, 1825; Henry I. Hunt, 1826; John Biddle, 1827; John Biddle, 1828; Jonathan Kearsley, 1829; John R. Williams, 1830; Marshall Chapin, 1831; Levi Cook, 1832; Marshall Chapin, 1833; Charles C. Trowbridge, 1834, resigned in August, and Andrew Mack elected to fill vacancy; Levi Cook, 1835; Levi Cook, 1836; Henry Howard, 1837; Augustus S. Porter, 1838, resigned in the fall, and Asher B. Bates, Recorder, acted; De Garmo Jones, 1839; Zina Pitcher, 1840; Zina Pitcher, 1841; Douglass Houghton, 1842; Zina Pitcher, 1843; John R. Williams, 1844; John R. Williams, 1845; John R. Williams, 1846; James A. Van Dyke, 1847; Frederick Buhl, 1848; Charles Howard, 1849; John Ladue, 1850; Zachariah Chandler, 1851; John H. Harmon, 1852; John H. Harmon, 1853; Oliver M. Hyde, 1854 and Henry Ledyard, '55.

SKETCHES OF THE CITY OF DETROIT.

Their business or profession and term of service were as follows:

John R. Williams, Merchant,	6 terms
Henry I Hunt, do	1 do
John Biddle, Officer U S A.,	2 do
Jonathan Kearsley, Officer U S A.	1 do
Marshall Chapin, Physician,	2 do
Levi Cook, Merchant,	3 do
C C. Trowbridge, Banker, Andrew Mack, seaman,	1 do
Henry Howard, Merchant	1 do
Augustus S. Porter, Lawyer, Asher B Bates, Lawyer,	1 do
De Garmo Jones, Merchant,	1 do
Zina Pitcher, Physician,	3 do
Douglass Houghton, Physician,	1 do
James A Van Dyke, Lawyer,	1 do
Frederick Buhl, Merchant,	1 do
Charles Howard do	1 do
John Ladue, Tanner,	1 do
Zachariah Chandler, Merchant,	1 do
John H Harmon, Printer,	2 do
Oliver M Hyde, Merchant,	1 do
Henry Ledyard, Lawyer,	1 do

Henry I Hunt died during his official term in '26, Marshall Chapin died in 1838, Douglass Houghton died in 1845, De Garmo Jones died in 1846, John Ladue died in 1854, John R Williams died in 1854, Andrew Mack died in 1854, and James A. Van Dyke died in 1855.

John Biddle is now sojourning in France, Augustus S Porter now resides at Black Rock, N. Y., Henry Howard in Buffalo N Y., and Asher B Bates in Sandwich Islands. Jonathan Kearsley, Levi Cook, Charles C. Trowbridge, Zina Pitcher, Frederick Buhl, Charles Howard, Zachariah Chandler, John H. Harmon, Oliver M. Hyde and Henry Ledyard, the present incumbent, all reside here.

POPULATION.

The population of the city proper returned in the spring of 1854, as taken by authority of the State, was 40,373 A population of 3,000 reside in contiguous city suburbs, which for all business estimates should properly be taken into account.

A portion of the population are foreigners, many of whom are uneducated, and do not speak English at all. They regard the operation of the census as a preparatory process to tax them according to their numeration, and it is now known that the census taken was quite below the true number. A full census of the city and suburb population, which are substantially one, would have shown a population of from 47,000 to 50,000 souls.

The population at the following periods, from 1820, was as follows:

In 1820 it was	1,442		
" 1830 "	2,222	—Increase in 10 years,	780
" 1840 "	9,102	" " "	6,880
" 1850 "	21,019	" " "	11,917
" 1854 "	40,373	" " 4 "	19,354

It will be seen that the population has doubled in the four years preceding 1854, and the water assessment just made shows that the ratio of increase has not diminished during the past year. The assessor found five hundred and seventy-five families residing in the city more than there were one year ago.

PROPERTY VALUATION.

The valuation of real and personal property assessed in the city in 1854 was	$12,518,115
Add for difference between valuation for purposes of taxing or of traffic	4,174,705
Add for real and personal property of railroads banks, &c., which pay a tax in gross to the State of one per cent. on their capital	3,500,000
Add for Church property not taxed	1,000,000
Public property not taxed waterworks engine houses, markets, public schools, &c. &c.	500,000
County and Central Government buildings	100,000
	$21,760,820

The following business statistics were returned with the census in the spring of 1854

The capital invested in manufactures within the city proper in 1854 was	$1,680,170
The products of the preceding year from manufactures were	$3,013,200
The value of merchandise imported in 1855 for the purpose of sale was	$7,422,700

PUBLIC DISBURSEMENTS 1853-4.

The disbursements for improvements and public purposes made in 1853 and '4 were, (excluding fractions) as follows

City expenditures in 1853 for interest, sewers &c.	$137,247	
City expenditures in 1854 for interest, sewers,	129,042	
" " 1853 public schools	9,956	
City expenditures in 1854 for public schools	10,164	
State and county tax paid by city in 1853 and '4	64,018	
Amount raised by general tax	$310,077	$310,070
Amount paid by special assessment in 1853 for paving streets	$61,710	
Amount paid by special assessment in 1854 for paving streets	67,311	
		129,021
Amount expended by Water Commissioners for re-constructing Water Works and contingencies in 1853	172,587	
Amount expended for same purpose in 1854	140,272	$312,859
City disbursements in two years		$751,956
Amount expended by Detroit Gas Light Company extending and enlarging their works in same time		100,000

Amount expended in erecting houses of public worship during the same time, as follows

Stone Presbyterian Churches	60,000
Brick "	50,000
Back "	40,000
Brick Congregational "	50,000
	$810,196
Amount of Water Loan	250,000
	$560,196
Amount drawn directly from sources of citizens	
Add for amount paid on subscription to Stock of Railroads, Plankroads, and other public improvements for same time	200,000
Shewing amount actually disbursed in the city from its own resources for public purposes, to be	$1,041,966

The amounts expended annually for paving streets, and other public improvements, thus enhancing greatly the value of property, is large, but is not more than is demanded by the rapid growth of the city. A public meeting held lately in pursuance of Mayor's proclamation voted to raise by tax the sum of $163,000 for public improvements the present year. This is in addition to the cost of paving, which will be at least half as much more, and is paid by special assessment.

LIABILITIES.

The city liabilities are Bonds due in 1855, $53,609; in 1857, $20,000; in 1858, $50,000; in 1859, $60,000; in 1865, $50,000; in 1869, $10,919; in 1870, $27,925, in 1871, $19,320; in 1872, $400, in 1873, $22,000; optional, $3,450;—Total, $317,632. These were issued for construction of the original Water Works, Public Sewers, City Hall, Markets, &c. &c., the payment whereof is provided for by the Common Council, and the interest on which is paid by direct annual tax.

By a law of the Legislature of the State, no further bonds for purposes of city improvements can issue from the Common Council, but all improvements thereafter to be made must be provided for and paid for by direct tax at the time of construction.

The law also requires a stated sum to be annually raised by tax, to go into a sinking fund pledged to the extinguishment of the public debt. Since the passage of the law, the sum of $35,199 38 has been placed to the credit of the public debt. This fund is computed to extinguish the above debt in seventeen years.

The Water Works liabilities are; Bonds due in 1873, $50,000; in 1878, $100,000; in 1880, $50,000; in 1883, 100,000; in 1885, $100,000; in 1890, $100,000;—Total, $500,000; $250,000 of which is now on hand to complete the re-construction of the works.

Total liabilities of city and water works $817,622.

In 1836, the total liabilities of the city were only $8,495.

The present debt of the city has since been created for the construction of water works, sewers, paving, public markets, &c, &c, besides some things less useful which it is not necessary now to recall—let by-gones be by-gones.

The largest portion of the debt contracted, has been applied to public improvements, imperiously demanded by the public weal. The public sewers—which improved property, checked disease, and so materially advanced the convenience of the public—need no defense.

The water works—the noblest improvements of our city—upon which its protection from fire, its health, its convenience, its comfort so much depends—are not too dear at any price, and which now will take care of the liabilities properly belonging to them.

The annual city tax has increased in ten years—from 1845 to 1855—from $19,000 to $163,000. The purposes for which the tax of the present year was levied, were as follows: Payment of interest $23,367; sinking fund $5,000; common schools $19,966; road tax $8,000; contingent fund $19,661; general fund $23,737; fire department $4,925; street lamps $1,000; general road fund $11,066; improvement of parks $1,200; sewers $38,960; site for Alms House $5,000; extension of market $2,100; payment on lot for city Hall $700; total $163,702. This sum, though large, was imperiously demanded in consequence of the rapid growth of the city and expansion of its improved limits, and was cheerfully voted and paid by our citizens, with commendable firmness and patriotism, rather than add to the public debt of the city, and they will continue to do so hereafter so long as it is necessary, for the improvement, health and prosperity of the city, and they are satisfied it is judiciously and honestly applied to the objects for which it is voted. The character and reputation of their city they prize above all other considerations, and will never suffer them to be tarnished.

The current expenses of the city in 1844–5 exclusive of interest paid, was $6,922.35, in the year 1854–5 they amounted, exclusive of interest and amount to sinking fund, to $105,519.94.

HOTELS.

The Hotels of Detroit are renowned for comfort, neatness and excellence of their fare. There are forty-nine hotels in the city, of various grades, several of which, usually denominated first class hotels, were designed and erected expressly for that purpose, and are large and extensive edifices, constructed in the most modern style with every modern improvement attached, affording to the sojourner every comfort, convenience and luxury. There are also a number of large taverns with extensive brick stables attached, designed and built expressly for the accommodation of farmers who come from a distance, bringing their produce to market with their own teams.

ARCHITECTURE.

In the erection of buildings, our citizens have generally been more solicitous of utility than ornament. Still we can point the stranger to some of the handsomest and most classic structures of modern times. The three Presbyterian Churches, one of stone, the others of brick, covered with mastic, and the Congregational Church, of brick and mastic, recently erected, are highly ornate, both exterior and interior, and almost stupenduously magnificent.

Besides these there are the Odd Fellows Hall, Firemens' Hall, Young Mens' Hall, Masonic Hall, U S Court House, Peninsular Bank, Savings Bank, St. Pauls Church, Mariners Church, Cathedral of St. Peter and St. Pauls, and 1st Methodist and Unitarian Churches and whole blocks of stores, which are fine specimens of architecture. There are also a number of private dwellings which are as fine specimens of the sublime art as any western city can boast of.

The Marine Hospital and Custom House and Post Office buildings soon to be erected by the General Government, and the Alms House and City Hall to be erected by the city, will be material acquisitions to our public buildings, and display of architecture.

PUBLIC GROUNDS.

The wide avenues and public parks and squares of Detroit, are evidences and enduring monuments of the wisdom, good taste and judgement of the Governor and Judges who devised and adopted the plan of the city, and elicit the enthusiastic commendation of strangers who visit us, which besides being adornments of an attractive character, are of vast utility in ventilating the city, and rendering it more salubrious, and in arresting the spread of fires. The Governor and Judges who adopted the plan, were as follows:

William Hull, Governor, Augustus B. Woodward, James Witherell and James Griffen, Judges.

The original plans were drawn in sections—12 in number, and each section signed by William Hull, Governor, and Peter Audrian, Secretary. The plan was designed and proposed by Judge Woodward and is commonly called "Woodward's plan" and it is fit and due to his memory that the most prominent public ground should bear his name, it is therefore proposed that Grand Circus, which is now divided into two parks, be by the Common Council hereafter designated by the name of "Woodward Parks."

Campus Martius, which is crossed by Woodward avenue, is 600 feet long and 250 feet wide, in the centre of which a fountain is to be placed at some future day.

The city has recently purchased from the State a large lot, on the west side of the square, with a front of 280 feet on Griswold street, for a site for the proposed City Hall, and on the east of the square is the Public Market extending down the centre of Michigan avenue, which avenue is 200 feet wide.

The Grand Circus which is also crossed in the centre by Woodward avenue, is a half circle, 500 feet across on Woodward avenue and 1000 feet on Adams avenue, on either side of Woodward avenue the grounds are enclosed, and set with trees, forming two parks. The water has been lately introduced into the centre of each of these, preparatory to the erection of fountains, which are to be immediately added, and the walks made agreeably to the beautiful plan which has been adopted, when the grounds will be thrown open to the public.

Centre Park is situated on the north side of State street, between Farrar and Farmer streets, and has a front on State street of 212 feet. It is enclosed and trees set, and is soon to be embellished with a fountain.

Capitol Park is situated on the north side of State street, between Griswold and Rowland sts, and has a front on State street of 168 feet. This park is enclosed, in the centre of which is the old State Capitol building, occupied by one of the Public Union Schools.

Besides the foregoing there is the east Park, surrounded by Farmer, Randolph and Bates sts, forming a triangle, with a front of 166 feet on either street, which is enclosed and trees set, and a fountain is now being placed in the centre.

The west Park is triangular, surrounded by State, Park and Palmer streets, with a front on State street of 168 feet. This Park has for many years been occupied by one of the Public School Houses, which is now to be removed, the ground enclosed and embellished with trees and a fountain.

North Park is triangular, surrounded by Randolph, Grand River and Centre streets with a front on Centre street of 80 feet; Crawford Park, at crossing of Fifth and Orchard street, is oblong, 140 by 144, Elton Park at crossing of Fifth and Oak street is oblong, 140 by 244 feet.

Besides the Parks, Washington avenue extending from Michigan avenue to the Grand Circus 1400 feet, is 200 feet in width, which is wide enough to admit of being parked 100 feet in the centre, and still leave ample carriage way on either side and also Madison avenue of the same width, extending from Randolph street to the Grand Circus 700 feet.

Should these two avenues be parked in the centre as proposed, they will in connection with the Grand Circus, form a continuous grand promenade, of more than half a mile in extent, from Michigan avenue to Randolph street.

A move has recently been made by our Common Council, to purchase a beautiful grove, embracing many acres of land on the Woodbridge farm, adjoining the west line of the city, north of Michigan avenue.

WIDTH OF AVENUES.

Washington Avenue,	200 feet
Jefferson Avenue,	120 feet.
Adams Avenue,	60 feet.
Madison Avenue,	200 feet
Monroe Avenue,	120 feet.
Woodward Avenue,	120 feet.
Miami Avenue,	120 feet
Macomb Avenue,	120 feet
East Michigan Avenue,	200 feet
West Michigan Avenue,	100 feet.
Cass Avenue,	100 feet.

Five of which bear the names of the five Presidents of the United States, who had occupied the chair, previous to the adoption of the plan, and their statues placed at the head of each of the avenues bearing their names respectively, would be an appropriate embellishment, and it is also suggested that the name of Campus Martius be changed to "Cass Square," and that a Statue of Gen. Cass be placed there. The streets are generally from 50 to 80 feet wide.

MERCANTILE.

Detroit, from its first settlement in 1701, has ranked first as a commercial point on the western Lakes. A company styled the "Company of the Colony of Canada," was incorporated by the Colony of Canada at a Convention held at Quebec, Oct. 31, 1701, which conferred upon them the right "to trade at Detroit in beaver and other peltries to the entire exclusion of all private individuals."

M. de La Motte Cadillac, the first commandant at Detroit who was commissioned by Louis XIV., in a letter to Count Ponchartrian in 1703, says, that his design in projecting the establishment of a trading post here in 1701, was to afford protection to commerce, since from this place we can go by canoe to all the nations that are around the lakes, it is a *door by which one can go in and out* to trade with all our allies. And we find that Charlavoix, a French Jesuit Missionary who visited this city as early as 1720, speaks of a complaint that the English merchants sell merchandize to the savages cheaper than the French do, thereby drawing all the trade to New York.

In 1787, that patriarch native citizen among us, who was born just after the close of the Pontiac war, Joseph Campau, Esq., actively engaged in the mercantile business here, and continued in it for about forty years. In early times he annually visited the city of Montreal, conveying in birch bark canoes cargoes of furs, &c., and returning with them freighted with goods.

Mr. Campau for many years had two stores, one where his present residence is, then the south side of St. Ann street, and the other on the river, a few rods above Ladue & Eldreds tannery. The old building was torn down a few weeks since.

The late Barnabus Campau, Esq, his brother, and the late Gen J. R. Williams, his nephew, were for many years employed by him as clerks, both of whom subsequently were engaged for many years in the mercantile business on their own account, and as well as Mr. J. Campau, accumulated large fortunes. It was not until about the year 1799 that any American merchants established themselves here.

In 1810 there were five or six merchants here, who imported their goods from the east, among whom were our estimable and enterprising citizen, Shubael Conant, Esq., and the venerable Joseph Campau, Esq., who are the only ones of that time now residents among us.

The books of Messrs. Mack & Conant, in possession of David Cooper, Esq., show that this firm imported their dry goods from England in 1818. The following price current for 1808 is made up from the account books of Thomas Emerson & Co., Merchants here at that time, which are also in possession of Mr. Cooper, who at that time was in the company's employ as book keeper.

Tea per lb 16s., Loaf Sugar per lb 3s. 6d., Brown Sugar per lb 2s. 6d.; Yellow Soap per lb 3s. 6d., Tallow Candles per lb 4s., Coffee per lb 4s., Pepper per lb. 5s., Cheese per lb 2s., Butter per lb 2s., Whiskey per gall. 8s., Boots per pair £10., Paper per quire 4s; British Sheeting per yard 6s. *Furs*—Raccoon 2s. 6d., Fox 2s. 6d., Otter 20s., Mink 3s., Cat 2s. 6., Muskrat 2s. 6., Beaver 24s. Oats per bushel 4s. Corn 6s. Flour per bbl. 14s. This firm shipped that year a large lot of flour to Fort Wayne, and paid 28s. per barrel, transportation on the same.

There are at this time three hundred and thirty-five stores of various kinds in the city. The stocks of merchandize formerly kept, were very much mixed, consisting of staple and fancy dry goods, groceries, iron and nails, crockery, hardware, leather, boots and shoes, hats and caps, clothing, &c., &c., "country stock."

But within a few years past business has become thoroughly divided, and we now have our exclusive dry goods stores, carpet stores, grocery stores, drugs and medicine stores, iron stores, hardware stores, crockery stores, leather stores, boot and shoe stores, hat, cap and fur stores, book stores, agricultural implements and seed stores, tea stores, wine and liquor stores, furniture stores, &c., &c., several of which confine themselves exclusively to the wholesale jobbing business.

Some of the dry goods stores are not equalled in the west, and excelled only by few in the east, in the beauty and magnificence of their buildings, in their internal arrangements, in the extent of stocks or amount of sales.

With the hope that it will not be considered invidious where there are so many extensive and well arranged dry goods, carpet and furnishing houses, the following description of one is ventured:

The store has a free stone front, is four stories high, occupies a front of fifty feet, and extending in depth one hundred feet, comprising ten rooms, each twenty-five feet in width and one hundred feet in depth, giving an area of 25,000 square feet, all of which are filled to their utmost capacity with foreign and domestic dry goods, carpets, cloths, millinery and clothing,—in addition to which the firm occupy a store-house in the rear. The retail rooms are four in number, finished in the most gorgeous style. About three hundred gas lights are required to light the several apartments. From sixty to seventy-five salesmen and from one hundred to one hundred and fifty persons altogether are employed in the several departments, and including those outside, seamsters and seamstresses, the firm give employment to about six hundred persons. Their invoices of merchandize imported during the year 1854 amounted to more than seven hundred thousand dollars.

This store was recently refitted and opened for the fall trade, with an invoice of goods amounting to over four hundred thousand dollars.

This is believed to be the most extensive and best arranged dry goods store in the United States, outside of New York.

Besides the numerous extensive dry goods and carpet and furnishing stores, there are several grocery, hardware, crockery, furniture, hat, cap and fur, boot and shoe and clothing stores, some of which comprise five rooms, twenty-five feet in width and two hundred feet in depth.

COMMERCE IN 1854.

The shipments from this port, by the Lakes and Canada Railway alone, during the year 1854, were in round numbers as follows: 337,000 barrels of flour, 897,000 bushels wheat 587,000 bushels corn, 5000 bushels rye, 2,500 bushels barley, 228,000 bushels oats, 1,800 barrels, and 1000 bags corn meal, 2,200 bags feed, 1,300 bags shorts, 40 bags buckwheat flour, 300 malt, 3000 bags and 480 bbls clover & grass seed, 380 bbls & 230 bags beans, 20 barrels peas, 194,500 bushels potatoes, 17,000 bushels turnips, 1,200 bushels onions, 24,600 barrels pork 18,600 barrels fish, 4,700 barrels beef, 450 barrels tallow, 6,000 barrels, and 226 kegs lard, 70 barrels and 2,300 kegs and firkins butter, 550 barrels eggs, 780 boxes and 38 casks cheese, 2,200 barrels and 157 sacks dried fruit, 340 barrels cranberries, 2,400 barrels and 73 sacks green apples, 27 barrels pickles, 230 barrels saur kraut, 300 barrels vinegar, 3,500 barrels beer, 7,680 casks highwines, 136 hogsheads and 1,193 barrels sugar, 460 barrels molasses, 2,350 packages tobacco, 870 kegs nails, 2,300 rolls leather, 17,000 hides, 1,600 bundles skins, 520 packs furs, 500 barrels oil, 1,900 casks ashes, 4,000 barrels water lime, 300 barrels plaster, 50 barrels cement, 9,500 barrels, and 1,900 bags salt, 62 barrels crackers, 117 barrels salts, 65 barrels saleratus, 1,000 barrels and 8 casks bees-wax, 50 packages and 30 tons game, 150 packs horns, 200 bales hair, 460 bales hemp, 39 bales ginseng, 380 bales broom corn, 570 fruit and ornamental trees, 100 horse rakes 300 stoves, 300 wheelbarrows, 70 carriages and wagons, 27 steam engines, 1000 empty half-barrels, 8,500 dressed hogs 80 dressed sheep, 9000 hams and shoulders, 480 tons iron, 240 tons hay, 1,500 live hogs, 7,000 head cattle, 3,000 head sheep, 22 horses, 550,000 lbs rags, 2,000,000 lbs wool, 119,000 lbs coal, 559 M staves, 4,600 M shingles, 9,000,000 pieces lath, 20,000,000 feet lumber, 940 tons ingot copper, and 14,000 tons unspecified merchandize.

This, exclusive of the amount distributed by other modes of transportation, such as the Michigan Central, and Detroit and Milwaukee Railroads, and other land carriage In the single article of stoves, stated above at the number of 300, the real total was actually over 5000

The receipts of general merchandize for the use of the city during the year, was 36,233 tons In addition, there was also received 9,000 barrels and 86,000 bags salt, 15,000 barrels water lime, 60 barrels stucco lime, 300 barrels cement, 15,500 barrels plaster, 336 tons crude plaster, 1000 tons pig iron 740 tons railroad iron, 2,500 tons coal 5,100 M shingles, 2,400,000 pieces lath, 10,000,000 feet lumber 80 tons hemp and 25 tons flax, (manufactured here into rope,) a consignment of furs direct from Russia, (invoiced at $2,200,) 1,400 tons copper ore, which, after being smelted here, yielded 946 tons pure ingot copper, equal to 66 per cent., and pine logs manufactured at the mills here into 36,000,000 feet of lumber, and 14,000,000 lath

	Number.	Tonnage.
The arrivals of American vessels in the coasting trade in 1854, were	2,290	1,006,850
Of Foreign vessels,	123	31,610
American vessels from foreign ports,	21	4,904
Totals,	2,434	1,043,494
The clearances of American vessels employed in the coasting trade were	2,494	1,200,892
Of foreign vessels,	16	37,786
Of American vessels foreign ports,	24	5,459
Totals,	2,534	1,244,137
The value of goods imported in American vessels was	946,985	
Of goods imported in foreign vessels,	27,721	
Total,	$1,014,706	
The amount of duties on merchandize imported was,	$111,578	
The value of exports of domestic produce to foreign ports in American vessels, was	118,401	
The value of exports of domestic produce to foreign ports in foreign vessels was	79,333	
Total,	$199,632	
The value of foreign goods exported was	66,135	
Total of exports,	$265,767	

The weight of merchandize of all kinds received at this port during the year, was one hundred and twenty-six thousand, seven hundred and eighty-one tons.

The number of passengers carried through the city by Michigan Central Railroad during the year 1854 was 451,689.

MANUFACTORIES.

It is not intended under this head to exhibit a complete view of Detroit Manufactories, giving facts and figures in detail, they not being at hand. But some of the departments of trade and industry are enumerated and sufficient to establish the fact that Detroit is a manufacturing, as well as a commercial city.

There are, within the city limits, 46 stationary steam engines, most of which are used in manufacturing establishments of various kinds, among them are ten iron machine shops, two locomotive manufactories, several brass foundries; sash, door and blind factories, tobacco and morocco manufactories and tanneries, others are used in saw-mills, flouring mills, plastermills, printing offices, breweries, &c. There are in the city 343 mechanic shops, among which are several iron foundries, boiler makers, blacksmith shops, carriage making, railroad car manufactories, furniture and chair, extensive boot and shoe and clothing establishments (several of which employ from one hundred to three hundred hands,) hat and cap manufactories and furriers, jewelers, church organ, piano forte makers, saddle and harness makers, copper and tin ware manufactories, stone and marble works, bakeries, lard oil, soap and candle manufactories, &c, &c,

Among the most important manufactures in the city is that of iron, which is now carried on the most extensively, employing as they do between one and two thousand men, and doing an aggregate business of over a million dollars annually.

The extensive mining and lumber regions of the north do now require all the steam engines, and other machinery that can be supplied from this point, while our increasing lake marine offers to our engineers a field for competition with the skill and capital of other cities. And here Detroit need have no apprehensions, as the works of past years sufficiently evince the superior skill of her mechanics, sending forth numbers of elegant low pressure engines, without a single failure.

The demand for engines will further increase with the development of the iron and copper mineral region of Lake Superior, now just rendered accessible, by the opening of the Sault St. Mary ship canal.

A rolling mill, prepared for every kind of work, up to the heaviest railroad iron, is very much required, and would without doubt prove a profitable investment.

The rich iron deposits of Lake Superior should be manufactured here at home into every form required. Now the large quantities of ore, or rather *pure native iron*, already produced, pass by us for want of works for its manufacture here, and near 1000 tons of which are returned in bars and sold and consumed here annually.

The copper smelting works here are altogether too small to smelt all the copper sent down to them, and large quantities are sent to works in other cities. The establishment here should be enlarged or a new one built without delay.

LUMBER.

Lumber is one of our great staples and must continue to be such for a long time to come, surrounded as we are with forests of pine, cherry, black walnut, oak, white wood and other timber.

The extensive forests of pine, covering a large part of our Peninsula, afford lumber of a superior quality, which is noted in all the principal markets.

The manufacture and shipments are mostly carried on along the St. Clair River, Lake Huron, and Saginaw Bay. There are, however, in the city and suburbs ten mills which manufactured during the year past 36,000,000 feet of lumber and 14,000,000 lath. Besides this there was received here from mills elsewhere 10,000,000 feet of lumber, 24,000,000 lath, and 5,100M shingles, making a total for 1854 of 40,000,000 feet of lumber, 38,000,000 lath, and 5,100 M shingles. This does not include any of that which arrived here over the plank-roads from the pine forests of Lapeer county, nor the large shipments made by our citizens directly from the pineries, where many of them own and manage mills. And one of our most extensive dealers estimates that the mills in this city will manufacture 50,000,000 feet of pine lumber the present season, ("Wights mill" alone, will make over 8,000,000 feet.)

The above represents only the trade in pine lumber, and does not include oak, black walnut, cherry and white wood, of which there are large quantities brought to this market and sold from the steam mills located at various points in the adjacent surrounding country.

WYANDOTTE.

This young city, bearing the name of the old Indian Chief, Walk-in-the-Water, after whom also the first steamboat which ever crossed Lake Erie was named, is situated on one of his favorite hunting grounds, on the bank of the Detroit river, ten miles below the city, and promises soon to become a large manufacturing place, and a valuable tributary to the business of this city.

A Stock Company recently purchased the "Biddle Farm," containing twenty-two hundred acres, from Major Biddle, the front of which embracing two miles on the river, and extending a half a mile back, has been dedicated as the site of the city of Wyandotte. Many lots have already been sold, and some thirty tenements erected.

The "Eureka Iron Company" who own extensive iron ore-beds on Lake Superior, design to bring down the ore and manufacture it into pigs at this place for which purpose they are erecting a blast furnace. Extensive coalprts are already set up, and a large amount of ore is to be brought down from the Lake this fall. The "Wyandotte Rolling Mills Company" are erecting very extensive works. Their main building is now in process of construction, the tin roof being nearly on. The building is one hundred and twenty feet square, twenty-nine feet between joints, and sixty-five feet to the top of the cupola, The rolling works are propelled by a large engine, taking its steam supply from five forty foot flew boilers, and the trip-hammer is worked by a separate engine,

The company have their machinery on the ground complete, for the manufacture of bar, roll, band and other iron. They have a heavy contract for the re-manufacture of railroad iron for the Michigan Central Railroad Company, upon which they will commence as soon as their works are in operation.

THE FISH TRADE OF THE LAKES.

The early French explorers of the upper lakes, in 1610 make mention of the white fish and trout as being very luxurious and much used for sustenance of life by the sons of the forest. From the time civilization dawned upon the shores of the lakes, the French settlers supplied themselves with them, and during the war of 1812, they were found of substantial benefit to our soldiers in appeasing their hunger, for the want of other supplies.

Previous to the completion of the Erie Canal, salt was mostly transported by the St. Lawrence and thence up the Lakes, and obtained only at enormous prices. After the canal was completed it became comparatively cheap, and Mr. Barnabas Compau, an enterprising merchant of the "olden time" was induced to pack a few barrels of white fish to ship to Buffalo for sale as an experiment. The experiment proved unprofitable, but Mr. Compau continued to pack annually until his death, which was in 1845. For many years the consumption was confined to Detroit and vicinity.

But in 1830 emigration to Michigan rapidly commenced, and increased to such a degree in 1834 that the new comers found it difficult to purchase produce, on account of the scarcity, as nearly everything consumed was imported from sister States. This caused a great consumption of fish, and gave birth to the extension of lake fisheries and several other grounds besides Mr. Compau's, which was on Belle Isle, (formerly Hog Island) owned by himself, and is still owned by his children,—it is situated a few miles above the city.

From this time the business increased and several grounds were cleared on the St. Clair River, and as the market increased they were extended to the shores of Lake Huron. Several houses in Detroit became extensively engaged in the business employing several vessels exclusively in the trade. The American Fur Company also engaged in it, and in 1841 two schooners were taken over the falls at the Saut St Marys into Lake Superior, for the purpose of fishing on that Lake.

Lake Superior abounds with the *siscowet*, a fish weighing from 8 to 10 pounds. They are exceedingly fat, and when tried will yield 25 per cent of oil.

There are a great variety of fish in the lakes, besides the white fish, siscowet and trout. Sturgeon weighing 120 pounds have been taken: trout 60 lbs, muskelunge 40 lbs, pickerel, 15 lbs; mullett, 10 lbs; bill fish 6, cat 25. In the vicinity of the Sault St Mary and all the streams emptying into Lake Superior, large quantities of small speckled or brook trout are taken.

In 1840 there were 35,000 barrels of fish of various kinds packed, and it is estimated that the quantity now annually taken cannot be less than 100,000 barrels. The most of which is brought to Detroit, where quantities are sold for home consumption; and market is found for them in Ohio, Illinois, and Indiana, and it is no uncommon thing to see them advertised in St Louis, Cincinnati, Louisville and Natchez; and on the other hand in New York and Boston, while they also show themselves at Salem, and Marblehead, the very head quarters of the mackerel fisheries.

The white fish is regarded as the prince of fresh water fish. Hon H R Schoolcraft in his poem, "the white fish" says:

> "All friends to good living by turene and del,
> Concur in exalting this prince of a fish;
> So fine in a platter, so tempting a fry,
> So rich on a gridiron, so sweet in a pie,
> That even before it the salmon must fall,
> And that mighty bonne-bouche, of the land beaver's tail.
>
> This fish is a subject to dainty and white,
> To show in a lecture, to eat or to write,
> That equals my joy, I declare, on my life,
> To raise up my voice, or to raise up my knife,
> 'Tis a morcel alike for the gourmand or faster;
> White, white as a tablet of pure alabaster!
> Its beauty or flavor no pen or I can doubt,
> When seen in the water, or tasted without,
> And all the dispute that opinion ere makes
> Of speaking of lake fishes, thus 'deer of the lakes,'*
> Pends not itself on oneness, to ponder or sup,
> But the best mode of dressing and serving it up
>
> * * * * *
>
> The muse might appeal to the science of books,
> To picture its ichthyological looks;
> Show what is its family likeness, or odds,
> Compared with its cousins, the salmons and cods;
> Tell where it approximates, point where it fails,
> By counting its fins, or dissecting the scales;
> O prove by plain reasons (such proof can be had)
> 'Tis not 'toothless salmon,' but rather lake shad.
> Here too, might a fancy to descant inclined,
> Contemplate the lore that pertains to the kind,
> And bring up the red man, in fanciful string,
> To prove its creation from feminine brains."†

*A translation of Ad-dik keem-maig, the Indian name for this fish.
†Vide 'Indian Tales and Legends.'

LAKE SUPERIOR TRADE.

The existence of Lake Superior was first known to the whites in 1641, when Charles Raymbault and Isaac Jogues, Jesuit missionaries, who first visited the Ste Marie river, were informed by the Indians that beyond the foaming rapids, was a lake called by them "Kitchi Gummi (Big Lake) and in 1660 Rene Mesnard a Jesuit Missionary, visited the lake and reached Point Keweenaw, who while crossing the Portage, wandered into the woods from his companions and was never heard of afterwards.

The importance of the mines of Lake Superior to the mercantile and manufacturing interests of Detroit has long been appreciated by its business men, who encouraged and assisted the hardy adventurers in successfully developing the country, and who advocated and procured the construction of the Sault Canal—a gigantic and almost imperishable work that must be ranked with the mighty structures of Greece and Rome. This great aqueduct was completed last spring, and Lake Superior the largest body of fresh water in the world, which has hitherto been navigated by only three or four inferior steamboats or propellers, that were taken over land around the falls is open to our lake commerce. A length of four hundred miles is thereby added to our inland navigation, which now extends uninterrupted from the Atlantic Ocean to the St Louis river, at the head of Lake Superior, in the territory of Minesota and Wisconsin. At which point a short line of railroad is soon to be constructed extending to the Mississippi river.

In the spring of 1845, the entire fleet on Lake Superior consisted of the schooners White Fish, belonging to the Hudson Bay Fur Company, the Siscowet, belonging to the A M F Co and the Algonquin, owned by Mr Mendenhall. During that year the schooners Napoleon Swallow, Uncle Tom Merchant, Chippewa, Ocean, and Fur Trader, were added, and in 1846, the steamboat Detroit was the first and only steamboat which plied regularly between Detroit and the Sault. Now there are four first-class passenger steamboats, besides several propellers running regularly between Detroit and ports on Lake Superior, passing through the Sault Canal.

The importations of provisions and supplies for the mines alone are more than a million dollars per annum, now, which will annually increase with the rapid settlement and development of the country.

LAKE SUPERIOR COPPER.

The existence of copper upon its shores appears to have been known to the earliest travelers and traders. As early as 1666, Father Claude Allouez visited the Lake, and informs us that pieces of copper were frequently found there, weighing from ten to twenty pounds.

In 1689, Baron La Hontan visited the Lake, and described the copper mines in his "Voyages to Canada." In 1721 P de Charlevoix passed thro the Lake on his way to the Gulf of Mexico, and mentions the copper mines in his "Journal of a Voyage to North America." Captain Carver visited the lake in 1766, and in his book of travels, published an account of the copper found on its shores. The mines were worked at as early a period as 1771, by a company composed of His Royal Highness, the Duke of Gloucester, Mr Secretary Townsend, Sir Samuel Tucket, Bart, Mr Baxter, Consul of the Emperor of Russia, and Mr Cruikshank, in England; and Sir William Johnson Bart, Mr Bostwick, Mr Baxter and Mr Henry in America. An air furnace was erected by this company at Point Aux Pin. Their mining operations were confined on the south shore of the lake, to the Ontonagon River. The object in forming this company was not for the purpose of obtaining copper, but for the silver the ore might contain. During the winter of 1771-2, they penetrated into the hill forty feet, on a vein of native copper, which held out that distance. In the spring, when the thaw came, the clay, on which they relied for its stiffness, and neglected to prop up, caved in. The enterprize was then abandoned. Traces of the early operations are distinctly visible at this late day, in the vicinity where the great copper rock weighing nearly two tons was found, which was removed by Mr. Julius Eldred of this city, in 1845, and now lies in the Navy Yard at Washington.

Dr. Franklin was familiar with the existence of these mines, who remarked that when drawing the treaty of peace with England in the city of Paris he had access to the journals and charts of a corps of French Engineers that were exploring Lake Superior when Quebec fell to the French; from which charts, he drew the line through Lake Superior, to include the most and best of the copper mines to the United States; that the time would come when drawing that line would be considered the greatest service he ever rendered his country, and the copper ore to be a greater source of wealth than any other nation possessed; that the facilities of transportation would be well improved, so as to export copper ore to Europe cheaper than they raised it from their own mines."

The first trace of any action of the United States Government, about the mines on Lake Superior, was during the administration of President John Adams. In 1800, Congress passed a resolution "respecting the copper mines, on the south shore of Lake Superior, providing that the President be authorized to employ an agent to collect information relative to the copper mines, whether the Indian titles to the lands subsisted, if so, on what terms it could be extinguished, &c.

In 1819 an expedition was fitted out by the General Government, under the command of General Cass, then Governor of the Territory of Michigan, for the purpose of settling existing difficulties among the various Indian tribes, living on the borders of Lake Superior and extending beyond the Mississippi River. Hon. Henry R. Schoolcraft accompanied General Cass, who collected a valuable mass of historical facts all tending to show the existence of Copper at many points, both on the main land and the islands.

In 1840 the State Geological Corps, under Dr. Houghton State Geologist, carried their researches into the wild, but interesting region of Lake Superior. The annual reports of Dr. Houghton contained a lucid statement of facts, giving extended and accurate information with regard to this interesting region, the knowledge of which had hitherto been confined to the imperfect and unlimited observation of voyaging travelers.

MINING.

Public attention had not been attracted to the mineral region of the Upper Peninsula of our State, and no attempt at mining there had been made since the suspension of operations by the English Company in 1772 until after Dr. Houghton commenced his Geological surveys of the region.

In 1842 a treaty was made with the Chippewa Indians, by Mr. Robert Stewart, of this city. By this treaty, all of the country east of Fondulac, including the islands in Lake Superior, not previously acquired, was ceded to the United States. Immediately after the ratification of the treaty in 1843, applications were made to explore and dig for Copper ore on the south shore of Lake Superior. The Secretary of war in the spring of that year, issued three permits to Ansley, to Wilson & Turner, and to Turner & Snyder. These were the first permits that were granted.

Shortly after Mr. Walter Cunningham was appointed Special Agent by the Government for the mines on Lake Superior, who established his agency at Copper Harbor. About this time Col. Chas. H. Gratiot, with a company of miners from the lead mines in Wisconsin, arrived at Copper Harbor, and commenced mining operations.

In 1844, C. C. Douglass formerly assistant State Geologist of Michigan, was employed by the Lake Superior Mining Company to explore their locations.

Dr. Houghton continued the Geological surveys of the region, until he lost his life, being wrecked in a storm on Lake Superior, on the 13th, of October 1845. Up to July 1846, about 900 permits were granted to different individuals, to work these mines, about 600 of which were located, and about 50 companies were organized under leases obtained from Government, and many commenced operations; several of which are in successful operation at this time. Among these are the Pittsburgh & Boston, (Cliff) Minesota, North American, Albion, North Western, North West, and Copper Falls.

In 1846, the committee on Public Lands made a report to Congress questioning the authority to grant permits and leases of these lands, and no further leases were issued. In 1848 Congress passed a law providing for the sale of these lands, and granting pre-emption rights. Several of the old Companies purchased the lands they had located under their leases, but most of them abandoned them, and but some five or six of the old Companies are now in existence. Other Companies were formed, who purchased mineral lands and there are now about 60 Copper Mining Companies organized, most of which are working their mines, others are exploring their tracts of land, and others again having mineral tracts of known value, which at present are inaccessable, are waiting the opening of roads to them, before commencing operations. Most of the Companies have hitherto prudently pursued the policy of working a small force on their locations, merely sufficient to explore, and gradually open and develope their mines, waiting the opening of the Sault Canal for the more vigorous and economical prosecution of operations. The opening of the Canal has given an impetus to mining operations this summer, and many of the young mines have increased forces working, and nothing but the most stringent condition in the financial affairs of the country prevents a much greater increase. The Lake Superior region already has a population estimated at 20,000, about equal to what there was in the whole Territory thirty years ago. Several thriving villages have sprung up, railroads are constructing, and a Locomotive of a large size is actually on its shores.

PRODUCE OF COPPER.

The first shipment of copper of any account, was made in 1818, amounting to about 200 tons. In 1853 there were 2535 tons of copper, of the value of $1,014,000 exported. In 1854 it is estimated that there were exported 3500 tons of copper valued at more than a million and a half of dollars, and it is estimated that the exports the present year will reach 5000 tons of copper valued at over two million dollars.

The Minesota mine is now producing about one hundred and thirty tons of Copper per month, and the Cliff mine about the same, making from these two mines alone, an aggregate of 3,120 tons of copper per year, which at $400 per ton—the estimated value at the mines, will produce $1,248,100.

Besides these, there are forty others of the younger mines, that will send forward from twenty to five hundred tons each, during the present year. The annual product of the mines will doubtless increase and double every two or three years for some time to come.

The shipments of copper from the Ontonagon district alone the present season up to August 18, amounted to 2,754,860 pounds, as follows:

Minesota and Rockland mines,	1,661,302 lbs
National,	56,369 "
Forest,	212,763 "
Norwich,	315,461 "
Ridge,	80,549 "
Nebraska,	37,600 "
Ohio Trap Rock,	42,733 "
Adventure,	91,470 "
Douglass Houghton,	50,145 "
Bohemian,	4,592 "
Toltec,	117,516 "
Windsor,	67,679 "
Evergreen Bluff,	14,690 "

The Minesota mine in the month of July produced 139½ tons, and will ship during the present season about 1500 tons of copper. The mines in the Portage Lake, and Kewenaw districts are equally productive, but not having them at hand, particulars are not here given

The total amount paid in by the share holders in the Cliff mine, (Kewenaw district) is $18,50 per share (on 6000 shares) and the company have realized from the product of the mine and divided $77 per share. The total amount paid in by the share-holders in the Minesota mine, (Ontonagon) is $22 per share, (on 3000 shares,) and the company have realized from the product of the mine and divided $60 per share. It will be borne in mind that all operations in Lake Superior, have hitherto been carried on at an enormous cost and every inconceivable inconvenience, and if such results were attained with all the embarrassments experienced, what may we not expect now that these embarrassments are removed; and mines hereafter will be developed for one-fourth the expense heretofore necessarily incurred.

All the copper of Lake Superior contains more or less native silver, and it is sometimes found in pieces weighing several pounds.

All of the Mines produce pure native copper, and masses weighing three and four hundred thousand pounds have been found.

Smelting works for the purpose of smelting Lake Superior Copper have been erected at Detroit, Cleveland and Pittsburgh, all of which are kept well supplied. The works at Detroit are the largest in the United States.

LAKE SUPERIOR IRON.

The following description of the iron ore of Lake Superior, was furnished by Charles A. Trowbridge, Esq., of Detroit, and first published in the transactions of the Agricultural Society.

"There is probably no part of the American Continent which can boast of as pure iron ore, in as great quantities, *entirely above the surface of the earth*, (the amount below the surface never having been ascertained) as the State of Michigan.

With regard to its purity, we quote a letter addressed to Edward K. Collins, Esq., by James R. Chilton, M. D. of New York City, in which Dr. Chilton says: "I give below the analysis of four samples of iron ore, which I took from boxes opened in my presence, at your office in Wall Street, each box being marked in accordance with the sample. The result was as follows:

Collins Iron Co., Iron Hill, on sec. No. 2.
Per oxyde of iron   92 26-100
equal to 6458-100 metalic iron.
  Silica   -   -   -   5 15-100
  Alumina   -   -   -   1 71-100
  Water & loss -   -   38-100
  Manganise—none.

  Making   -   -   -   100 00 p'rts

Messrs. Trowbridge & Graverats Iron Hill sec No 10.
Per oxyde of iron,   94 37-100
equal to 6606-100 metalic iron
  Silica   -   -   -   3 11-100
  Alumina   -   -   -   1 44-100
  Manganise -   -   -   16-100
  Water and loss -   92-100

  Making   -   -   100 00 parts

Jackson Iron Co., Iron Hill on sec No 1.
Per oxyde of iron,   95 60-100
equal to 6692-100 metalic iron.
  Silica   -   -   -   1 71-100
  Alumina   -   -   -   1 54-100
  Lime and Manganise -   43-100
  Water and loss -   -   72-100

  Making   -   -   -   100 00 parts

Christaline ore from Messrs Trowbridge and Graverats Iron Hill on sec No 10.
Per oxyde of iron,   98 78-100
equal to 6915-100 metalic iron.
  Silica   -   -   -   46-100
  Alumina   -   -   -   13-100
  Water and loss -   -   62-100

  Making   -   -   100 00 parts

Each of the above samples was tested for *Phosphorus and sulphur*, but without detecting any; therefore I know of no reason why these ores should not yield iron of the very best quality, by the simplest mode of reduction.

Respectfully submitted,   JAMES R. CHILTON."

We will here remark, that the boxes of ore mentioned by Dr Chilton, were taken from the top of the iron hill mentioned by Mr Collins, in the summer of 1853; and the verbal opinion expressed by the Doctor, at the time he made the analysis, was that the ore must increase in richness as you descend towards the base of the hill. As these "iron hills" are from 150 to 300 feet in height, and one solid mass of "iron" there can be but little doubt, but that at a depth of 100 feet from the surface, the ore must yield nearly 80 per centum metalic iron

Some of the hills above mentioned, are 80 rods in length by 40 rods in width, containing millions upon millions of tons of this very rich ore

As regards the quality and strength of the iron made from this ore, we quote from the report of Major Wade of the United States Ordnance Department, made to the Secretary of War. Senate Documents, Special Session, March, 1851. page 80

Strength of pounds per square inch
Iron from Salisbury, Conn, by means of
40 trials	58,009
" from Sweden 4 trials,	58,184
" from Centre County, Pa, 15 trials,	58,400
" from Lancaster " " 2 "	58,661
" from McIntyre, Essex County, N. J, 4 trials	58,912
" from England, Cable Bolt, E. V, 5 trials,	59,105
" from Russia 5 trials,	75,069
" from Carp river, Lake Superior,	89,582

By the above data it will be seen that the Lake Superior iron sustained a pressure of 13,513 lbs. more to the square inch than Russia iron, which was found to sustain 16,694 more per square inch than English cable bolt, which is known to be the strongest iron England makes; thereby showing the Lake Superior iron to be about 54 per cent. stronger than the best English cable bolt. This iron has been so thoroughly proven in New York, Boston, Pittsburgh, Cincinnati, and at the United States Navy Yard, within the past five years, by manufacturing it into car axles, boiler plate, steam engines, wire, tacks, nails, (the cut nail being found to clinch as well as the ordinary wrought nails) and the manufacture of steel, that a volume could, if necessary, be written to show its great strength and tenacity. All that is now wanted, is a sufficiency of capital to transport the ore to market, or manufacture the iron with charcoal, in the immediate vicinity of the "hills" where there is a superabundance of the best water power in the State: and we can see no reason why Michigan cannot supply her sister states with this superior iron at a lower price than any other iron can be produced in this country. Bloom iron can be made with charcoal in Marquette county, by water power, and placed on board vessels at the low price of $26,50 per ton of 2 240 pounds; and the same iron can be sold in New York, for $100 per ton for the various purposes we have enumerated—the ore being above the surface, its value can be as easily ascertained as the value of a pine tree in the forest; and investments of capital in this business, do not run that hazard they necessarily must run in seeking for copper and other materials below the surface.

We consider that a trip to the Iron Hills of Lake Superior will more than pay any one, if he does nothing more than take a hasty survey of that immense mineral deposite, without investing a farthing in the various adventures to make them productive."

Works for the manufacture of Iron are now in operation at Marquette, and others are being erected, Railroads from Marquette to the Iron manufactories have been constructed, and the whistle of the Locomotive is already heard there, while large quantities of the Ore are transported to Erie, Cleveland and Wyandotte, a few miles below Detroit, to be manufactured.

The "Collins Iron Company" have erected very extensive works at Marquette. and have recently commenced the manufacture of bar iron, and their first shipment of 62 tons was received here a few days since. They now have four forges, and will in a short time have eight in operation, when they will manufacture 50 tons per week. This iron on account of its superior quality, sells readily for one hundred dollars per ton.

Since the above was written, another shipment of 200 tons of bar iron has been received.

LAKE SUPERIOR MARBLE.

In the vicinity, and beyond the 'Iron Hills,' extensive beds of superior Marble have been found, but for the want of roads they are at present inaccessible. But this will in a short time be remedied when these quarries will be worked, and the time is not distant when it will be used in Detroit for building purposes, and Marble Palaces will be erected by the "Mining and Manufacturing Princes" of the Upper Peninsula.

No estimate could easily overvalue the richness and importance of the traffic of the Lake Superior region, even now, and Riches that make the almost fabulous wealth of Australia and California but insignificant lie buried beyond the iron and copper bound shores of the Lake.

COAL.

About 100,000 tons of Mineral Coal is annually consumed in Detroit by manufactories, Furnaces, Gas Works and Steamboats and for domestic purposes. All of which is at present brought here from Ohio and Pennsylvania, while within a distance of less than 100 miles from the city, extensive fields of superior quality, of coal have been known to exist for many years past, but which could not be made available to us for want of a cheap mode of conveyance to this point. This is now soon to be afforded by the construction of the Detroit and Milwaukee Railroad, which passes directly through the coal district, when it is expected that our own coal fields will not only supply coal for the consumption of the city but also the mineral region of the Upper Peninsula, at cheaper rates than it can be obtained from any other source.

The late Dr. Houghton, State Geologist, made thorough explorations of the coal districts, and in his reports to the Legislature in 1839, 1840 and 1841, he says that the main bed of coal which traverses the central counties of the State has been traced northerly to within a few miles of the south line of Shiawassee county, and that the bed has been found of sufficient thickness to admit of being profitably worked." Also "south-westerly into Jackson county, where the bed is of sufficient thickness to admit of being worked, and the coal is of a quality well fitted for all the purposes to which that substance is applied."

"The most extensive beds of coal were noticed in township 4 north, range 1 and 2 east, in Ingham county, and range 3 and 4 west in Eaton county. "A bed of bituminous coal more than 2 feet thick of a superior quality in town 4 north range 2 east occurs in the bed and banks of Cedar River, Ingham county. It is compact, has a glossy lustre, ignites easily, burns with a light flame, and leaves only a small quantity of earthy residue." After commenting on the 'range and extent of the coal bearing rocks' he says "On the east group of rocks appears in the towns of Leoni and West portage, in Jackson county, in the north east corner town of Ingham county, in the bed of the Red Cedar River.

Its boundary is known to stretch northerly across the Shiawassee and Flint Rivers, thus bringing within the limits of the coal rocks, parts of Genesee, Shiawassee, Ingham, Jackson, Calhoun, Barry and Kent Counties, and probably the whole of Eaton, Ionia and Clinton Counties." "The coal at this point (Red Cedar River, Ingham county) is very accessable, and must ere long prove of great importance."

"The coal has here (Shiawassee County) a thickness of from three and a half to four feet."

From these extracts it appears that the coal bearing rocks extend through nine counties of the State, (and they probably do more,) a distance of nearly one hundred miles and that the same stratum of coal, belonging to the lower coal basin, is exhibited to view at three different points of out crop, viz. at Barry, in Jackson county, at Red River, in Ingham county, 35 miles from Barry, and at Shiawassee River, 25 miles from Red Cedar River, occupying a line at least 60 miles in extent.

Col. Richard R. Lansing, President of the Michigan Coal Company, who has spent the past ten years in investigating and exploring the coal fields, says that in 1844 he sank a shaft at Red Cedar river, through the coal bed which at that point was about seven feet below the surface, and that he found it to be two feet nine inches thick, overlaid by a stratum of fire clay, and resting on a bed of stone. That in 1850 he caused another shaft to be sunk, and the actual measurement of the thickness of the coal bed at that point, as reported to him, was found to be 2 70-100 feet

In 1853, Col. Lansing laid bare the coal bed at Red Cedar River, to the extent of upward of a thousand superficial square feet, and removed to the surface about 60 tons of coal. The structure varied in thickness from three feet to twenty-eight inches. 14 tons of the coal was transported to Detroit, to be subjected to all the tests for the various purposes for which bituminous coal is generally used, which was tested by Mr. S. H. Newhall, Superintendant of motive power M C. R. R., who certified to its adaptation for forges. Mr. Eber B Ward who had its power to raise steam, tested on one of his Boats, testifies that "the coal burned freely, emitting a great deal of flame and raising steam rapidly, was reduced to ashes without exhibiting any evidences of Sulphur, or clinker, or making any impression on the grates of the furnaces, which after the experiment, were left as free from any adhesive matter as if wood had been burned.'

Col. Orville B. Dibble of the "Biddle House," after testing it in making Gas, certified that his "decided opinion is, your coal yields as much gas as any other domestic coal used for that purpose, and its luminous qualities certainly exceed any other gas manufactured by us."

Mr. Francis Smith an Engineer of great experience, in the making coke in the north of England, certifies that he made some experiments with the "Michigan Coal and came to the conclusion, which was entirely favorable to the coal as being good for the making of coke, that he "had seen a gas retort charged with this coal three several times, and the coke yielded in these instances, was, throughout, of that uniform silvery appearance which is an invariable feature in good coke," and, that his impression is, "that this coal with proper ovens, would make as good coke as that now used in England, in firing Locomotives and blast furnaces."

For domestic use Adrian R Terry M. D, certifies that he "never in the Western country, burnt a coal which gave so clear and brilliant a flame and of which the coke, (after the bitumen was burned out,) made so permanent and hot a fire. It leaves but an insignificant amount of ashes or earthy residue, in comparison with any coal I have ever burned in this region"

The foregoing certificates are published in the "Transactions of the Michigan Agricultural Society"

The Coal fields belonging to the "Michigan Coal Company" which is now fully organized, are three in number. One upon the Michigan Central Rail Road, one upon the Detroit and Milwaukee Rail Road and one upon the Detroit and Lansing Plank Road. Each of which have recently been explored by Mr. A. G. Bradford, of Pennsylvania, a scientific gentleman of high attainments, and each is spoken of in a report made by him to the Board of Directors, in the most favorable terms. Mr. B. states at the conclusion of his report, that "The Coal found at each place is of extraordinary purity, approaching in quality 'Cannel Coal' blending in its component parts, all the necessary elements for every variety of use. From my Coal explorations in several States of the Union, to which I have devoted the most of my attention for the past fifteen years of my life, I can safely say, that I never saw Coal at the out crop of such extraordinary quality and purity, and so free generally from Sulphur and other impurities."

This Company is about commencing active mining operations.

SALT.

It is estimated, that there is annually brought to this State $400,000 worth of salt from the New York Salt Springs. This should, and the time is not distant when it will be manufactured and supplied from the salt springs of this State, which are known to produce brine of sufficient strength and purity for profitable manufacture.

Bela Hubbard, Esq., late assistant State Geologist, in a communication to J. C. Holmes, Esq., Secretary of the State Agricultural Society says, "The State Geologist early pointed out the fact of the existence of large salt deposits and indicated the points at which borings might be most profitably conducted. These were commenced in 1839 at Grand Rapids and Tittabawassa river. Owing to the great expense and difficulty at that time of obtaining the necessary materials for the undertaking, no sufficient appropriations were made and the works were abandoned when the borings had proceeded to not more than half the depth indicated as that which would be found necessary, the last being estimated at from 600 to 700 feet. Even at the depth reached on Grand River (about 300 feet) the quantity and strength of the brine discharged, exceeded that obtained at any of the Salt Springs in the country, except those of New York, being not less than 130 gallons per minute of which about 100 gallons contained a bushel of salt. At the same time, a private enterprise, undertaken at Grand Rapids, by the Hon. Lucius Lyon, had conducted borings to a depth of 400 feet, yielding a brine, when the upper fresh waters could be shut off, of which, about 28 gallons contained a bushel of salt. None of these borings however, had extended into the lower salt rock a sufficient depth to reach the strongest brine, and the great difficulties attending the work in connection with the small facilities for securing a market and for competition with the rich salt springs of western New York, induced a temporary abandonment."

Facilities for procuring proper materials for working and for conveying the salt when manufactured to market, will now soon be afforded by the completion of the Detroit and Milwaukee Railroad, and these salt wells will again be opened, and to the proper depth indicated by Dr. Houghton, when it is confidently expected that the brine produced, will be second in character to none in the United States.

CITY STATISTICS, 1855.

The following is a recapitulation of the statistics of the city, prepared and reported to the Board of Water Commissioners by their Secretary, June 30th, 1855, at which time the city contained:

Families,*	6,329	Bakeries,	21	Public Markets,	2
Offices,	175	Dye Houses,	5	Soap and Candle factories,	9
Boiler Manufactories,	4	Churches,	28	Public St. Sprinklers,	2
Saw Manufactory,	1	Hospital,	1	Groceries,	260
Tanneries & Morocco facts,	7	Private Schools,	24	Iron Founderies,	7
Potteries	2	Rail Road Depots,	2	Steam planing door sash, blind and furniture factories	12
Soda & Small Beer Factories,	5	Breweries,	17		
Jail,	1	Malt Houses,	2	Burr Mill Stone factory,	1
Fire Engine Houses,	9	Boarding Houses,	131	Water Works.	1
Private Meat Markets,	24	Taverns,	49	Public Halls,	9
Stone and Marble Works,	10	Iron Machine Shops,	10	Theatres,	2
Stationary Steam Engines,	46	Locomotive Manfactories,	2	Public Schools,	25
Rectifying Distilleries,	2	Flour Mills,	3	Warehouses,	24
Stores,	335	Steam Tobacco Factories,	6	Lard Oil Factory	1
Mechanic Shops,	343	Gas Works,	1	Wheat Elevators	2
R. R. Car Factories,	2	Printing Offices,	11	Public bathing establishments,	4
Saw Mills,	6	Banks,	4		
Plaster Mill,	1	Orphans' Homes,	2		

*This number more properly represents the number of House keepers than the number of families. The number is made up from those assessed for water, and where families are boarding with others

SKETCHES OF THE CITY OF DETROIT.   31

The above includes those only within the city limits while within a mile above and below there are, say 709 families, several saw mills, tanneries, breweries, a copper smelting works, dry dock, &c., &c., all of which are to be taken into account, when estimating the business &c. of the city.

The number of families residing in the several Wards of the City, July 1st 1855, were as follows—	
First Ward	667
Second Ward	229
Third Ward	560
Fourth Ward	977
Fifth Ward	817
Sixth Ward	1,159
Seventh Ward	1,065
Eighth Ward	854
Total	6,328

The number of families residing in the lower or western district of the city, comprising the 1st, 2d, 5th and 8th Wards, was, 2,597
The number of families residing in the upper or eastern district, comprising the 3d, 4th, 6th and 7th Wards, was, 3,731.

The increase of number of Families in the City, for the year ending July 1st, 1855, was as follows—
In the lower or western district, comprising 1st, 2d, 5th and 8th Wards, as follows—

First Ward	14 Families.
Second Ward	5 "
Fifth Ward	87 "
Eighth Ward	97 "
Total	203 "

In the upper or eastern district, comprising the 3d, 4th, 7th and 6th Wards, as follows,—

Third Ward	1 "
Fourth Ward	34 "
Sixth Ward	164 "
Seventh Ward	173 "
Total	372 "
Total increase in City,	575 "

SCHOOLS---THEIR EARLY HISTORY.

The compiler of these sketches is indebted for the following sketch of the early history of schools in Detroit, to Hon. B. F. H. Witherell, to whom the public are frequently indebted for interesting sketches of the early history of Michigan, published in the city papers.

DEAR SIR:—At your suggestion, I send you a sketch of the early history of Schools in our Territory, so far as I have been able to learn it.

It is difficult to trace in detail, the efforts made more than a half a century since for the education of our people—shut out as they were, from the rest of the civilized world, by hundreds of miles of pathless forests, and scattered along the margins of our rivers and lakes, of whom some few hundreds only were gathered about the hamlet of Detroit—then only a trading post, with a garrison to protect it.

On enquiry of some of the "Old Settlers," I learn, that some time during the latter part of the last century, Monsieur Recours, and afterwards Mr Ballpour taught 'the school.' and after them, about 1799 to 1803, a Mr. Burrel wielded the ensign of authority. he kept on St. James street in the rear of the present Freemason's Hall.

After Burrell, came Mr Donovan. He taught at the Park-house, between St. Louis st., and the river, in rear of Palmer & Whipples' Stationer's store.

On the 11th of June, 1805, in the morning when the fire burst out, (which consumed every house in the town, but one) one of the scholars tells me that he was in school—hearing the alarm, the boys all rushed forth to see the fun; but while in full career, they were suddenly arrested, by a cask of tamarinds, thrown into the street from a burning store, on which they feasted till the flames drove them off. Teacher and scholars in a few minutes found themselves, hatless and bookless—all were consumed—and the whole town being in ashes, none could be got. But the old French fashion of making a turban of a handkerchief, answered the purpose.

Old John Goff, the old sage, with his drab breeches and long blue stockings, followed Donovan. He kept "the school" for several years after the fire. The boys say that he

or in boarding houses and taverns, they are not set down. The number of families boarding is unusually large at present in the city, in consequence of the scarcity of dwellings to rent, the assessor found but 23 in the whole city at the time he went through it, and he passed through every street. And several of these were vacant to repair. This number of families he estimates would average, including single persons, (of which there is a much greater proportion than in eastern cities,) and the families boarding, at eight each, which would give a population at that time in the city of 50,634.

had not the fear of the Maine Law before his eyes, but daily got a little *corned* in the forenoon, and *licked* the boys, and in the afternoon, *kissed* the girls. At last the old man passed away from mortal ken—having taught as long as he could stand on his legs.— He first opened his school on the west side of the mouth of the "River Savoyard," near the old residence of the late Col. D. G. Jones, and his last school was kept opposite B. Thompson's Livery Stable.

"The River Savoyard" somewhat noted in the annals of our city, was nothing more than a large creek, draining the common back of the town and a few farms lying above it. It was sometimes a large stream, and I have known it necessary to take people living along its margin, out of their windows into a canoe and carry them *ashore*. This was after long-continued rains; but our modern subterranean rivers have done the work for "the Savoyard"—its glory is departed—it is "among the things that *were*' but are not.

It obtained its name from old Peter Berthlett; (the grand-father of those yet among us,) he kept a pottery on the west side of its mouth, near the outlet of the present grand sewer. He bore the nick-name of "Savoyard' probably because himself or his ancestors were from Savoy, he always went by that name. Mrs Sheldon has in some way transformed it to "Xavier," which it never bore.

Old Father Berthlett went to Montreal, and in days when stoves were a scarce article, brought up a large number, and let them out for from three to ten dollars each, per winter, and by this and other operations, became the wealthiest man in Canada. He died about thirty years ago.

"Mais revenon a nos Mouton."

Daniel Curtis kept "the school' a while in 1810 and '11. He was then appointed an officer in the army, and a right brave and gallant soldier he was. He, and a brother Lieutenant, in spite of the orders of a drunken Captain, held out for many days against a large body of Indians who besieged Fort ——, until relieved by a body of General Harrison's light-horse.

Old Mr Rowe next entered the field after the war was over, and taught "the school" in a little wooden building, which stood in the rear of Ives' Broker's office, in Griswold street, belonging to Joseph Compau. Here the sciences flourished under the influence of the old man's birchen rod. There was a little cupola on the edifice—the only one of the kind west of Lake Erie. The young ideas rapidly expanded under its shadow. Rowe slept with his fathers, and as all things must have an end, so did the cupola. Griswold street was to be widened. Mr Compau refused his assent, and deeming the offered compensation insufficient, he refused to remove the building, and the agents of the city *sawed down* through it and sold that part that was in the street to John Farmer (I think) who yet owns it.

The good old Father Richard, the only Catholic clergyman in the country—whom none knew but to respect—was anxious to educate his people, and about the year 1811, sent to France and procured M. Le Salliere to come over as a teacher. He taught a short time, but the war came on and his school ceased. There are yet several men among us, who owe much of their scholastic knowledge to Father Richard's personal attention as their teacher, but his clerical duties, occupied too much of his time to leave as much as he desired for educational purposes.

Among the well educated men—natives of the country in olden time, was that sterling old patriot, Captain Charles Morau, the father of the Judge.

When quite a young man he was employed in the office of Captain Phillip de Jean, so well known, and who figured largely in the history of Michigan, some eighty years since. De Jean was an emigrant from France, and was appointed a magistrate by the British Lieutenant-Governor Hamilton, under whose orders, he, on the 18th of March, 1776, tried John Contencinan for stealing some beaver, otter, and raccoon skins, from Abbot & Finchly, and Ann Wylie, formerly a slave of Abbott & Finchley on a charge of stealing *or being accused* of stealing a purse containing six guineas, &c. The sentence of Justice de Jean was, that they be "hanged, hanged, hanged, and strangled till they be dead on the king's domain," (the common); and they *were* hanged. Governor Hamilton and de Jean soon after left on a military expedition to "the Illinois," where they were made prisoners by Gen. George Rogers Clark, whom the State of Virginia had sent over the Alleghanies with a small force to protect the infant settlements of the west.

Hamilton and De Jean never returned; had they done so, they would have been tried for murder—as the Governor-General and Chief Justice had caused warrants to be issued from Quebec for their arrest. "HAMTRAMCK."

COMMON SCHOOLS.

The Common Schools of Detroit, where every child in the city can obtain the elements of a good English Education *free of charge* are the pride and boast of our city.

Common Schools were first established in 1842. Previous to this time but little interest had been manifested in the cause of general education, and the first to take the initiatory steps towards the establishment of a system of general education was Dr. Zina Pitcher, who, while Mayor in 1841, called the attention of the Common Council to the great need of Common Schools in the city. A report was subsequently made to the Council which showed there were 27 English Schools, 1 French and 1 German School in the city, and the whole number of pupils about seven hundred, while there were upwards of two thousand children of the proper school age in the city.

Measures were then immediately taken to establish an additional number of Schools, and seven others were soon opened, and urgent efforts used to persuade parents whose children were then roaming the streets, to send them to these Schools. In 1842 an act was passed by the Legislature incorporating the various Schools of the city into one District, under the style of the "Board of Education of the City of Detroit." The Board is composed of two School Inspectors from each ward, one of whom is annually elected for the term of two years.

Dr. Pitcher, distinguished and beloved for his untiring efforts in behalf of every interest connected with the cause of Education in this city and state, both as a member of the Board of Education and Board of Regents of the State University (of which until recently he was a member from its first establishment,) continued his efforts in behalf of the Common Schools without abatement and while Mayor presided over the deliberations of the Board, and zealously devoted himself to develope and perfect the Free School System.

Dr. Pitcher had in the late Hon. Samuel Barstow an able and devoted coadjutor. Who from their establishment up to the time of his death (which took place July 12th, 1854,) was unwearied in his efforts, devoting much of his time and talents to perfect the system, and establish the Schools on a permanent basis.

To the persistent, unwearied and united exertions of Dr. Pitcher and Mr. Barstow, the system in a great degree owes its present perfection. Other members of the Board deserve honorable mention for their early efforts in behalf of the cause of Education, among whom are George Robb, D. Bethune Duffield, Eben N. Wilcox, James V. Campbell, and Charles Byram, Esqs.

Mr. Barstow was President of the Board for many years, and was succeeded by Levi Bishop, Esq., the present able and efficient incumbent, in whom the cause of Education has a worthy successor of the lamented Barstow.

The Schools under the charge of the Board, are three Union Schools; two Middle Schools; eleven Primary Schools and one Colored School. The three Union Schools contain eleven departments, and have an aggregate attendance of 2,000 Scholars.

The number of teachers employed in all the Schools, is thirty seven, of whom nine are males, and twenty eight are females. The number of Scholars in all the Schools, during the past year was 5000. The expenditures for the year amounted to 16,623.94. The value of the property owned by the Board is estimated at thirty-five thousand dollars.

The Schools are sustained by moneys annually drawn from the State School Fund, and by a tax on the real and personal property in the city.

It is in contemplation to establish at an early day, a High School, where pupils may be prepared for the University Course. When this is done the system will be complete in form, and if carried out with the same faithfulness that has hitherto characterised the acts of the Board, the pupils in the Detroit Common Schools will rank favorably with those of any other similar institution in the country.

Besides the Common Schools, there are twenty-four private Schools and Seminaries in the city, where those who wish can educate their children; and two excellent Commercial Colleges.

Since the foregoing was prepared, the proceedings of the Board of Education contain the following:

On motion of Levi Bishop, the following preamble and resolutions were unanimously adopted:

Whereas, The late Samuel Barstow, Esq, once President of this Board, was, from the beginning, one of the most efficient and active promoters of the free school system of Detroit, and its present state of prosperity and increasing usefulness is in a large measure due to his untiring zeal and self denying labors; therefore,

Resolved, That the newly enlarged school building in the Seventh Ward be named in his honor the "Barstow Union School," and that the Building Committee cause a marble tablet to be inserted in the vacant panel in the front of said building, inscribed with the words "Barstow Union School."

CHURCHES AND RELIGIOUS SOCIETIES.

The first house for public worship erected in the city, was built by the Roman Catholics, in the year 1723, on a site now occupied by Jefferson Avenue, and directly in front of the Masonic Hall and was burned with the city in 1805. The Cathedral of St. Ann, erected on the triangle, between Larned and Congress, and Bates and Randolph streets, was commenced in 1817 by the Rev. Gabriel Richard, but was not completed until after his death, in 1832, though it was occupied by the Society for many years before.

The first Protestant Society in Detroit, was organized by the Methodists, in 1812.

The first Episcopal Society was organized in 1824.

The first Presbyterian Church was organized in 1825—which society erected a house of worship on the corner of Woodward Avenue and Larned street, where the brick church, afterwards erected by them was burned in January 1854. The church was constructed of wood, and was removed to give place for the brick one, and is now owned and occupied by the Irish Catholic Society, and is located on the corner of Porter and Sixth streets, and is shortly to be removed to give place for a more commodious brick edifice.

There are at this time 28 church edifices in the City, as follows:

ROMAN CATHOLIC.

Cathedral of St. Ann, (French) cor Bates and Larned streets—stone.

Cathedral of St. Peter and St. Paul (Irish) corner Jefferson Avenue and St. Antoine streets—brick.

St. Mary's Church, (German) corner Croghan and St. Antoine streets—brick.

Trinity Church, (Irish) corner Porter and Sixth street—wood.

PROTESTANT.

Presbyterian Church, corner State and Farrar streets—brick.

Presbyterian Church, corner Fort and Fourth streets—stone.

Presbyterian Church, corner Jefferson Avenue, near Rivard street—brick.

Presbyterian Church corner Lafayette and Cass streets—brick
Presbyterian Church (Scotch) East Park—wood
Congregational Church, corner Fort and Wayne streets—brick
St Paul's Church corner Congress and Shelby streets—stone
Christ's Church, Jefferson Avenue, between Hastings and Rivard—wood
Mariner's Church, corner Woodward Avenue and Woodbridge street—stone
St Mathews Church, (colored) corner Congress and St Antoine street—wood
Baptist Church, corner Fort and Griswold sts —wood
Tabernacle, Baptist, Howard, between Second and Third streets—wood
Methodist church, corner Woodward Avenue and State street—brick
Methodist church corner Congress and Randolph streets—brick
Methodist church corner La Fayette and Fourth streets—wood
Methodist church corner of Walnut and Seventh streets—brick
Methodist church, (French) corner Rivard and Croghan streets—brick
Methodist church, (German) corner Croghan near St Antoine—brick
Methodist church (colored) La Fayette street, near Beaubien—brick
New church, corner Jefferson Avenue and Beaubien street—brick
Unitarian church, corner La Fayette and Shelby street—brick
Dutch Reformed church corner Congress near Rivard street—brick
Dutch Reformed church corner Croghan and St Antoine streets—brick
German Lutheran church, corner Monroe Avenue and Randolph streets—brick
Four stone, eighteen brick and six wood

Several religious societies destitute of houses of worship hold service in public halls, &c

Many of the Churches are elegant and costly edifices. The Church of St Ann (French Catholic) is the oldest church in Detroit. It is 151 feet long and 60 feet wide. The Cathedral of Saints Peter and Paul (Catholic) is the largest, being 160 feet in length, 81 feet wide and 72 feet high. The steeple, which is not yet erected, is designed to be 200 feet to its top from the pavement.

The Congregational and three Presbyterian Churches, erected within the past two years, are large and commodious, each capable of seating 1000 persons, and are not surpassed in their style of architecture in the western States. They were all designed and constructed under the superintendence of Mr A Jordon, architect of this city. The following is a description of one of them just completed.

The Fort Street Presbyterian Church is built of limestone, from the quarries at Malden, in the early decorated style of Gothic architecture. It has the principal tower on the north-west corner, with small tower on the north-east corner and a square tower in the centre of front gable. The face work is of rubble stone, laid in even courses, having the pinnacles, moulded jambs, tracery, and other trimmings, of cut stone. The main tower is 100 feet high, and has heavy projecting buttresses on the corners, finishing against the belfry story in an octagonal form, and continued up above the parapet with crocketed pinnacles. The spire rises to the height of 130 feet above the tower, octagonal in form, and enriched with boldly carved crockets on the angles. From the pinnacles on the four corners of the tower spring flying buttresses to the corners of the spire, pierced with pointed openings, and having crocketed parapets. The front is richly decorated with tracery, the hoods to windows crocketed, the gable surmounted with embattled parapet, a niche on either side of centre window, the centre tower finished with a pierced parapet, and richly crocketed pinnacles. The small tower terminates with a two story lantern, each story pierced with eight openings.

The audience chamber is 90 feet long by 60 feet wide, lighted by six pointed windows on each side, and a circular window in the rear wall. It has an open roof, supported by six trusses spanning across the building, elaborately filled with tracery up to the ridge, which is 72 feet high above the floor. The back wall is ornamented with a handsome screen, having an overhanging canopy above the pulpit richly carved and decorated.

There are no galleries, except the one for the choir, which is over the vestibule, and in which is placed a fine organ, built by Mr. George Stevens, of Cambridge, Massachusetts, at a cost of $4,000. There are twelve chandeliers in the audience chamber—two suspended from pendants of each roof truss—forming a pleasing *coup d'œil*. There are a centre and two side aisles to the church, and one hundred and ninety slips, capable of seating 1,000 persons. The basement story is 12 feet high, containing a lecture room, which will seat 400, Sabbath and infant school rooms, pastor's study, two furnace and fuel rooms.

The cost of the edifice and its finishings is $70,000. It has been built from the designs of Messrs O. & A. Jordan, of this city, under the superintendence of Mr A. Jordan The contractors were, for the mason work, Mr Thos. Fairbairn; carpenters' work, Messrs McDuff & Mitchell; plastering Messrs. Rowe & Boyd; painting, Messrs Godfrey, Dean & Liable. The furnaces were furnished by Messrs. Dudley & Holmes.

CEMETERIES.

The first Roman Catholic Cemetery was situated where the Masonic Hall, now stands; and was used as such from 1723 until the year 1810, when the Governor and Judges granted to the corporation of St Ann, the public triangle in section one for the purpose of erecting a church thereon, and sixteen city lots north of the same for a burying ground.

Here the remains of Col. Hamtramck repose. His tomb bears the following inscription:—

"Sacred to the memory of John Francis Hamtramck, Esq., Col. of the 1st. U. S Regiment of Infantry, and commandant of Detroit and its dependencies. He departed this life, on the 11th of April, 1803, aged 45 years 7 months and 28 days. True patriotism and zealous attachment to national liberty, joined to a laudable ambition, led him into military service at an early period of his life. He was a soldier even before he was a man.

He was an active participator in all the dangers, difficulties and honors of the Revolutionary War. And his heroism and uniform good conduct, procured him the attention and personal thanks of the immortal Washington. The United States in him have lost a valuable officer and a good citizen, and society an useful and pleasant member. To his family the loss is incalculable; and his friends will never forget the memory of Hamtramck. This humble monument is placed over his remains by the officers who had the honor to serve under his command, a small but grateful tribute to his merit and his worth."

This ground was used until about 1826, when the Society purchased a lot on the Antoine Beaubien farm, near the Gratiot road, for a Cemetery; and interments were made there until about the year 1846, when they purchased a large and handsomely located lot of land in the town of Hamtramck, about two miles above the city, which is called "Mount Elliott." The Protestant burying ground in an early day, was on the north side of Larned street, and east of Woodward Avenue, now occupied by the Holmes' Block, Water Works' Office, &c.— The military burial ground occupied most of the square formed by Fort, Shelby, Lafayette and Griswold streets. No interments were made there after 1827; and in 1828, on removing the Fort, the remains were taken up and removed to a new ground. The burial ground on the corner of Larned Street and Woodward Avenue, continued to be used until about 1826, when the city purchased a lot adjoining the Catholic ground, on the Antoine Beaubian farm; and also in 1834, about fifty acres of land for a cemetery on the Gouin farm, north of the Gratiot road, part of which was laid out into small lots and sold. This ground is still used as the City burial ground.

ELMWOOD.

This beautiful and sequestered Cemetery lies in the Township of Hamtramck, about two miles from the City Hall, and occupies about sixty-five acres of land, well diversified, of light and porous soil, well adapted to its design.

The ground was purchased in the spring of the year 1846. The fit improvements, such as fencing, laying out drives and walks, and platting into lots, proceeded during the summer; a tasteful English Cottage, designed as a residence for the Superintendent, was erected, and in October of that year, it was opened for the interment of the departed It afterwards became incorporated by act of the Legislature. The following persons constituted the first Board of Officers elected under the act of incorporation, viz:

A. D FRASER was elected President, JOHN OWEN, Treasurer, HENRY LEDYARD, Secretary; HENRY LEDYARD and CHARLES C TROWBRIDGE, Executive Committee.

The following is the list of original subscribers:

Douglass & Walker John A. Welles, Henry H. Brown, H. P. Baldwin, Henry Ledyard, Geo. E Hand, J M. Howard, Franklin Moore, Hallock & Raymond, A W Buel, George F. Porter, J S. Farrand, George Foote, C. C. Trowbridge, John Owen, F. Buhl, W A. Raymond, J N Elbert, D Smart, C. Morse, J. A Van Dyke, H. H. Emmons, J S. Jenness, Edward Lyon, Harmon DeGraff, Samuel Coit, Shubael Conant, S P. Brady, Frederick Wetmore, J. W Tillman, E Farnsworth, George C Bates, Charles S. Tripler, W. N. Carpenter, A. S. Kellogg, E. Eldred, Z. Chandler, D. Cooper, J. G. Hill, G. R Russell, A. S. Williams, A. H. Adams, C. H. Avery, George Hill, John Drew, E P. Hastings, C. Howard, C G. Hammond, A. S Porter, T. Romeyn, A D Fraser, J. F Joy, W. Truesdill, J. Winder, E. A. Wales, James V Campbell, Darius Lamson, J. A. Hicks, Luther Beecher, M F. Dickinson, Henry Doty, Samuel Barstow, Thomas W Lockwood, Richard H. Hall, Pierre Teller, D Goodwin, B F Larned, Robert Dermont, DeGarmo Jones, Michigan Lodge No 1. by A. S Kellogg, Wayne Lodge No. 2 by A. S, Kellogg, Wawe-a-touong Lodge No 12 by A. S Kellogg, Moses P. Hutchins, J H Farnsworth, Alexander Goodell, T. H Hinchman, William S. Lee, Bela Hubbard, A. Clark, J. L. King.

Since the original purchase, twenty-five acres has been added, on the N. W side, extending along upon the sides of the ravine, adding largely to the interesting feature, and capabilities of the place.

Here, beneath the shade of the old towering elms, whose name it bears, will sleep, as they pass away, the generations who have peopled Detroit.

> "Here on this spot,
> Where many generations sleep forgot,
> Upf um M rble tomb and grassy mound,
> There cometh on the ear a peaceful sound,
> Which bids us be contented with our lot,
> And suffer calmly."

The mild breath of Spring blows gently across the grave of youth and beauty, the gorgeous summer comes up and stands in her pride around the tomb of maturity, and the wind of autumn sighing drearily, scatters the yellow leaves over the last resting place of those who have gone down in the fulness of years, and winter comes, last in its time, clasping all like death itself, in its dumb cold embrace.

If it indicates a gentle spirit, and hearts open to the influences of elevated humanity to cherish and beautify the graves of lost love—to honor the useful and good, and to freshen the remembrance of the sweet and lovely in life, then has Detroit furnished such evidence in her chaste, secluded, picturesque and beautiful Elmwood.

WATER WORKS.

A supply of pure water is essential to the health, and therefore to the prosperity of any city. The citizens of Detroit may well congratulate themselves upon having a water works, which furnishes an abundant supply of as pure water as any in the world, conveying it into their very dwellings, and at rates far cheaper than any other city. The water is taken from the river above the city and forced by two steam engines into an iron reservoir 60 feet in diameter and 20 feet deep, elevated on a circular brick tower 50 feet in height from which it is distributed throughout the city, by means of iron and wood pipes.

The soil upon which the city is built, being mostly impermeable clay, the water procured by wells, is, with occasional and few exceptions, surface, and not spring water, and contains a large per cent of organic matter, greatly increased in the neighborhood of drains and sewers, and which therefore constitutes a serious objection to its use. Its analysis showed that it contained 116 grains of compound ingredients to a gallon, while a gallon of water taken from these works exhibited but about 5 grains; the compound of the river water being composed mostly of silica, allumina, and iron, elements that can produce little or no injury; while the solid matter of the well water contained a large quantity of chloride of sodium, chloride of potassium, and magnesium, the two latter being cathartic in their properties. The analysis also shows that the water of the river, drawn from the great northern lakes, and from which the works are supplied, is found as pure and free from mineral substance as almost any body of water in the world.

In 1836, the city purchased the works, which had been established by individual enterprise, ten years before, and expended upon them about $120,000. In 1852, at which time they had cost the city the sum of $266,000, over and above all receipts, they were placed under the management of a board of Trustees who were subsequently, by act of the Legislature, incorporated as a board of Commissioners. Up to the 1st of January last the Commissioners had expended in reconstructing and enlarging the works, the sum of $271,000. The amount of their ordinary receipts over ordinary expenditures was $41,600—making the amount expended for construction over receipts $229,400, which added to the amount before expended by the Common Council, shows the total cost of the works to January 1st, 1855, to be $495,400.

In 1838, when the works were first regularly conducted by the city, the assessments amounted to $3,676, and the number of assessments to 613. In 1847 the assessments were $9,488, and the number was 1,251. In 1854, the assessments were $31,840, and the number was 5,872. The assessment of 1854 exceeded that of the previous year by more than $3,000, and the assessment for 1855, is $36,184—being an increase of $4,344 over last year, and 663 more families are supplied with water from the works, than there were one year ago; while there is no doubt that this ratio of increase will continue for many years, on the lines alone of pipes now laid. There are now 27 miles of iron and about 14 miles of wooden pipes. It would be a low figure to estimate the amount of assessment from the pipes now laid at $50,000 annually, when the lines are filled by buildings—an event, at the present rate of construction, not far off. The extension of pipes will at the same time be required in new districts which are fast being settled. There are now at least one thousand families living beyond the reach of water from these works, who procure but a scanty supply from wells.

The population of the city having doubled in the last four years, and the receipts for water nearly so, it would be safe to estimate that the population and receipts for water will double in the next five years. So that by the time the loan recently made, of $250,000 is expended in extending the works, the revenue from the water would not only pay the annual interest and ordinary expenses, but leave a large surplus annually to go into a sinking fund pledged to the extinguishment of the debt.

The works are owned by the city, and managed by a Board of Commissioners, chosen by the Common Council. The water rates are not fixed by any law, but are graduated by the Board to meet the requirements properly belonging to them.

The present minimum price for families, is four dollars per annum, a fraction over *one cent per day* which it is believed, is lower than that established by any other water works in the union. The project of supplying the inhabitants with water, by means of water works was agitated at an early day. In 1820 a proposition was made to the Trustees by Mr. John W. Tomkins to furnish the city with water, but no action was had on the proposition by the Board, except ordering it placed on file, though subsequently frequent discussions were had. Nothing decisive was adopted until 1825, when a Water Works was commenced by Mr. Bathuel Farrand under an act passed by the Common Council granting him "the sole and exclusive right of watering the city," and in 1827 the citizens were first furnished with water from the works. The water was raised by two pumps of 5 inches bore, driven by horse power into a forty gallon cask, at the top of a cupola, from which it was conducted through tamarack logs to a reservoir 16 feet square and six feet deep, situated on the lot now occupied by the Firemen's Hall, corner of Jefferson Avenue and Bates street. The pump was at the foot of Randolph street, on lot 25, Berthelet's subdivision, adjoining French & Eldred's Carding Mill. In 1829 other parties became interested in the works, and a Company was organised under an ordinance passed by the Common Council, which company was subsequently incorporated by the Legislative Council. The company made an effort to obtain a supply of water by boring into the earth in 1829, and bored a hole of four inches in diameter to the depth of 260 feet, on a lot at the S E. corner of Fort and Wayne streets, ten feet of alluvial earth was first passed through, next a stratum of tenacious marly clay with veins of quick sand 115 feet, 2 feet of beach sand with pebble stones succeeded and rock was then struck. It consisted of a stratum of graduiferous lime rock 60 feet in depth. The anger then penetrated sixty-five feet into lias, in the course of which it fell into a cavity 2¼ inches in depth. A stratum of carbonate of lime impregnated with salt, in a rather friable and yielding form succeeded, which was considered a subordinate bed in the lias, for the latter was again found below it, and the boring continued eight feet, when no water was obtained and the project abandoned.

In 1830 the Company constructed a reservoir 18 feet square and 9 feet deep on the same lot. The water was pumped into it by means of a ten horse power engine, driving a rotary pump, and was forced through a three inch iron pipe. The Company continued to extend their works and made every effort to supply the inhabitants with water in the face of an increasing pecuniary loss and the complaints of the public, until 1836, when they were purchased by the city. The city projected the present works, and the construction commenced in 1837. In 1841 the "New Works" were so far brought into use as to supply water to the Fort Street reservoir. In 1842 the present iron reservoir was brought into use, and the Fort Street reservoir abandoned. The works were conducted by a Superintendent annually appointed by the Council, until the Spring of 1849, when he was elected at the Charter Election. For several years there had been many complaints of an irregular and insufficient supply of water, and discussions and debates were had as to the best policy to be pursued. Many were in favor of the sale of the works. In February 1852 the Common Council passed an ordinance by which the control and management of the works were vested in a Board of Trustees, and Shubael Conant, Henry Ledyard, Edmund A. Brush, James A. Van Dyke and William R. Noyes, were appointed Trustees. The Board at once determined to re-construct the works on an enlarged scale. In the mean time relief was afforded to several sections of the city by the extension of iron distribution pipes.

In February 1853, an act was passed by the Legislature, incorporating the 'Board of Water Commissioners of the City of Detroit," and naming the gentlemen who composed the Board of Trustees as Commissioners with power to loan $250,000. The Board of Commissioners was organized on the 16th of May following, the loan was soon affected, and the money obtained, when the work of reconstruction commenced, and seven and a-half miles of iron pipes were laid, fifty-four new fire hydrants erected, and twenty-nine stop cocks put in before the close of the season. The Board also purchased 10 acres of land on the Dequindre farm, on the summit, north of the Gratiot road, about one and a-half miles from the river, for the purpose of constructing thereon a new reservoir.

NEW RESERVOIR.

In 1854 the work was resumed, and the construction of a new reservoir commenced, and about one-third of the work accomplished during the year. The reservoir is to be constructed in two basins—by raising earth embankments to a height of thirty feet. The embankments are to be 103 feet through at the base, and 15 feet at the top, in the centre of which a puddled wall 16 feet at the base, and 8 feet at the top. The slopes of the embankment outside are to be sodded and set with evergreens, and inside first lined with concrete and then paved with brick. A flight of stone steps will be built on the inside slope of either basin from the terrace to the bottom. The terrace on the top to be gravelled, and a fence constructed on the inner side around the basins. Either basin will be 200 feet square at the top, 114½ feet at the bottom. The two basins covering nearly 4 acres. The top water line will be 50 ft. above the intersection of Jefferson and Woodward Avenues, and 77½ feet above the river. The total storage of the two basins will be 7,592,704 imperial gallons. The terrace at the top will be reached by a flight of stone steps; at the base, one or more fountains will constantly jet forth streams of water. When completed, it will afford a commanding view of the city and surrounding country, and a delightful promenade for pleasure.

The water is to be forced up to the reservoir by a powerful cornish steam engine, through an iron pipe, 24 inches interior diameter. The water will be distributed through a 24 inch pipe, extending from the reservoir to the western line of the city, connecting with all the pipes in streets running at right angles from the river. A stand pipe is to be erected at the engine house wharf, inside of a brick tower, 115 feet in heigh. The top of the tower will be reached by a flight of stairs inside around the pipe. The top of the tower will be about forty feet above the reservoir, and afford a fine view of the City, Lake St. Clair and surrounding country.

When the summit reservoir is completed, it is contemptlated to abandon the use of the one at the river.

It is expected that the new works will be entirely completed within the next two years and it is estimated that the Board now have the necessary amount of money to accomplish it. They having recently negociated a further loan of $250,000 under authority of an act of the Legislature passed February 6 1855.

During the year 1854 the present works distributed 314,392,655 gallons. The greatest number of gallons distributed in any one month was 33,498,222 and the works now being built are designed to be capable of supplying 3,000,000 gallons in twelve hours, equal to 90,000,000 gallons per month.

Hon. James A. Van Dyke, a zealous and efficient member of the board, from its first organization, and who for many years previous was intimately connected with our city affairs, as City Attorney, Alderman, Mayor of the city, and President of the Fire Department, and thoroughly acquainted with all the concerns of the community, and devoting much of his time and talents, devising and forwarding plans which have from time to time been adopted for advancing the prosperity of the city, was removed by death on the 8th day of May 1855.

Hon. Alexander D. Fraser, on whose report to the Common Council while Recorder of the city, in 1836, the city purchased the water works, was appointed a Commissioner by the Common Council to fill the vacancy occasioned by the death of Mr. Van Dyke. The following gentlemen now compose the Board of Commissioners: Edmund A. Brush, Shubael Conant, Henry Ledyard, Alexander D. Fraser and William R. Noyes, and the Officers are Edmund A. Brush, President, R. E. Roberts, Secretary, and Jacob Houghton, Jr., Superintendent and Engineer.

SKETCHES OF THE CITY OF DETROIT.

The following statement shows the increase of Assessments from year to year since the purchase of the Works by the City, and is designed to show the growth of the City, and increasing demand upon the Works rather than the Revenue

The assessments for the year 1838, 1839, and 1840, were irregular, one year running into the other. The aggregate amount of receipts of those years was $11,030 00 or an average of 3,676 66
Assessment of 1841, amounted to............ 5 446 00
" 1842, " .... 5,686 00—increase of......... $ 240 00
" 1843, " .... 7,163 18 " 1,477 18
" 1844, " .... 8 710 50 " 1,547 32
" 1845, " .... 9,488 34 " 777 84
" 1846, " .... 10,396 00 " 907 66
" 1847, " .... 9,832 18—decrease of......... 563 82
" 1848, " .... 10,738 00—increase of......... 905 82
" 1849, " .... 12 633 00 " 1,895 00
" 1850, " .... 15 612 00 " 2,979 00
" 1851, " .... 19,756 00 " 4 114 00
" 1852, " .... 25,348 00 " 5 592 00
" 1853, " .... 28,617 00 " 3,269 00
" 1854, " .... 31,840 00 " 3,223 00
" 1855, " .... 36 184 00 " 4,344 00

Increase of the number of Assessments for the past ten years

	Assessments in 1845	Assessments in 1855
Families,	915	5,282
Taverns,	23	48
Stores Offices and Shops,	215	1,028
Railroad Depots,	2	3
Breweries,	2	17
Stationary Steam Engines,	2	40
Mills, Factories, &c.,	92	222
Total,	1,251	6 640

COMPARATIVE PURITY OF WATER.

The following table shows the solid matter in a gallon of water taken from lakes, rivers and wells, in different cities:

LAKES AND RIVERS.	Grains solid matter	WELLS.	Grains solid matter
London, { Thames River,	28,000	Paris—Artesian Well,	9,860
{ New River,	19 200	New York, { Manhattan Well,	125,000
New York—Croton River,	6 998	{ Average several,	58,000
Albany—Hudson River,	6,320	Albany, { Lydius Street Well,	19,240
Troy, N. Y.—Mohawk River,	7,880	{ Old State House Well,	36,000
Brooklyn—Average Long I. Ponds,	2,367	{ Exchange Well,	64,680
Boston—Cochituate Lake,	1,850	{ Capitol Park Well,	65,520
Bridgeport, Ct.—Pequomock River,	0,992	Brooklyn—Average several Wells,	48,833
Philadelphia—Skuylkill River,	4 260	Boston, { Beacon Hill Well,	50,055
Rochester, N. Y., { Hemlock Lake,	1,330	{ Tremont Street Well,	26,600
{ Lake Ontario,	4,160	{ Longacre Well,	56,800
{ Genesee River,	11,210	Rochester, N. Y—Average several,	30,000
Cincinnati—Ohio River,	6,736	Detroit—Park Lot Well,	116,461
Detroit—Detroit River,	5,722		

Of the Detroit river water, Prof. Douglass, in his report of the analysis, says: That it contains less solid matter in the gallon than either the Croton or Cincinnati water, but more than the Fairmouth or Long Pond water. In estimating the value of your city water, as compared with water of other cities, due allowance must be made for the fact that the total solid matter is materially increased by the presence of silicia, allumina, and iron, elements that can produce little or no injury; while the chlorides, much the most injurious compounds, are entirely absent. The presence of such large quantities of silica and iron, is accounted for by the fact that Lake Superior and Huron are formed, for the most part, in a basin of ferruginous sandstone and igneous rock.

Of Detroit well water, he says The large quantity of chloride of sodium, (common salt,) chloride of potasium and magnesium found in it, clearly indicate its surface origin The two last salts are cathartic in their properties, and the habitual use of water, holding them in solution, in any considerable quantities, must prove injurious to health.

HEAD OF WATER.

The theoretic head of water, in various localities, from the present reservoir when it is full, is as follows

At the corners of	feet	At the corners of	feet
Jefferson Ave. and Third street,	63	Woodward Ave. and Atwater street,	60
" " Cass street,	48	" " Woodbridge st.,	51
" " Wayne street,	41	" " Jefferson Ave.,	40
" " Shelby street,	38	" " Larned street,	42
" " Woodward Ave.,	40	" " Congress street,	46
" " St. Antoine street,	39	" " Fort street,	43
" " Hastings street,	37	" " State street,	40
" " Rivard street,	34	" " Clifford street,	43
" " Russell street,	40	" " Circus street,	41
" " Riopelle street,	42	" " Adams Avenue,	34
" " Orleans street,	45	" " High street,	34
Fort street and Eighth street,	47	" " Sibley street,	29
" " Sixth street,	45	" " Toll gate,	14
" " Fifth street,	43	" " North city line,	10
" " Fourth street,	41	Lafayette street and Eighth street,	41
" " Third street,	39	" " Seventh street,	40
" " Second street,	35	" " Fourth street,	38
" " Wayne street,	32	" " Cass street,	35
" " Shelby street,	33	Michigan Avenue and Seventh street	42
" " Griswold street,	37	" " Third street,	45
" " Randolph streets,	48	" " First street,	42
Gratiot street and Randolph street,	39	" " Shelby street,	40
" " Beaubien street,	40	" " Griswold street,	39
" " Hastings street,	37	" " Bates street,	46
" " Rivard street,	29	Congress street and Seventh streets,	51
" " Russell street,	25	" " Sixth street,	52
" " Orleans street,	21	" " Fourth street,	53
Brush and Macomb streets,	39	" " Third street,	51
" " Gratiot street,	40	" " First street,	47
" " Columbia street,	34	" " Wayne street,	45
" " High street,	29	" " Griswold street,	47
Orleans and Atwater street,	64	" " Bates street,	43
" " Woodbridge street,	54	" " Brush street,	45
" " Jefferson Avenue,	45	" " Beaubien street,	44
" " Larned street,	44	" " St. Antoine st.,	45
" " Croghan street,	41	" " Hastings street,	46
" " Mullett street,	36	" " Russell street,	44
" " High street,	28	At Grand Circus,	40
" " Gratiot street,	21	" Centre Park,	38
" " Scott street,	18	" Capitol Park,	40
" " Hale street,	17	" West Park,	44
" " St. Joseph street,	15	" East Park,	43
" North Park	41	" Crawford Park,	41
" Campus Martius	43	" Elton Park,	34

Corner Sixth and Grand River sts, 33.

GAS LIGHT.

Detroit is well lighted with Gas, which is supplied by an incorporated Company, who have erected very extensive works on the river, near the eastern line of the City. Gas pipes extend through most of the principal streets, at present, and the Company are constantly extending them into new districts. There are already over twelve hundred Street Lamps set, for the purpose of lighting the city at night and we *now* wonder how they got along at night, in cities without gas.

PAVEMENTS AND SEWERS.

All the Streets and Avenues in the business portion of the city are paved with stone, making in the agregate about 13 miles of paved streets, and, the work of paving is progressing, and will continue until every street is paved.

A proper system of sewerage is of vital importance to the prosperity of any city. As a preventive of sickness, as a matter of economy and comfort addresses itself to every citizen. The subject engaged the early attention of the authorities of the city, and a large stone and brick sewer was constructed along the track of the creek which formerly run through the low grounds between Jefferson Avenue and Fort street. Since which time a number of sewers have been constructed in various sections of the city. The sewers are constructed of brick, and are circular, from 3 to 5 feet diameter. They are constructed by the city, and paid for out of a fund raised by general tax for that purpose, and premises drained into them, subjected to an annual 'Sewer Tax."

PLANK ROADS.

There are seven Plank Roads leading from the city into the country, the aggregate length of which is about 300 miles, they are

The Detroit and Grosse Point, Detroit and Erin, Detroit and Birmingham, Detroit and Howell, Detroit and Saline, Detroit and Monroe, Detroit and Plymouth.

THE RIVER.

The Detroit River is 25 miles in length, between lakes St Clair and Erie, average width one mile, depth 6 fathoms, current 2 miles an hour, and it is estimated that at this velocity at a transverse section, opposite the city, where it is contracted to about 52 chains it discharges 190,270,080 cubic feet per hour, or 3,171,168 cubic feet per minute.

There are seventeen islands in the river. The names of these are, "Clay," "Celeron," "Hickory," "Sugar," "Bois Blanc," "Elba," "Fox," "Rock," "Stoney." "Grosse," "Turkey," "Fighting," "Mammy Judy," "Grassy," "Mud," "Belle" and "Peach." The two latter are situated a few miles above, and within sight of the city, near the entrance to Lake St Clair The largest of which is Belle Isle (formerly Hog Island) Peach Island was the home of Pontiac. Parkman in his "History of the Conspiracy of Pontiac," says, " Pontiac, the Satan of this forest paradise, was accustomed to spend the early part of the summer upon a small island at the opening of Lake St. Clair, hidden from view by the high woods that covered the intervening *Isle au Cochou.

"The king and lord of all this country," as Rogers calls him, "lived in no royal state. His cabin was a small, oven-shaped structure of bark and rushes. Here he dwelt with his squaws and children; and here, doubtless, he might often have been seen, carelessly reclining his naked form on a rush mat, or a bear skin, like an ordinary warrior."

The other fifteen islands are situated within the first twelve miles of the river, after entering it from Lake Erie, some of which are in view of the city. The largest of which is Grosse Isle, on which are a number of large and well cultivated farms. This island is a very popular retreat for citizens of Detroit during the heat of summer. On some of the others there are extensive stone quarries; and on many of these, as well as Belle Isle and Peach, are extensive fisheries, where large quantities of white fish are annually taken. Father Hennepin who was a passenger on the "Griffin," the first vessel that crossed Lake Erie, in 1679, in his description of the scenery along the route, says, " the islands are the finest in the world; the strait is finer than Niagara; the banks are vast meadows and the prospect is terminated

*Now Belle Isle.

with some hills covered with vineyards, trees bearing good fruit, groves and forests so well disposed, that one would think that nature alone could not have made, without the help of art, so charming a prospect." The streams emptying into the *strait*, are, on the Canada side, the river aux Canards, and on the American shore, the Huron river, Monquagon creek, river Ecorse, river Rouge, May's creek, below the city, and Bloody Run and Connor's creek above

The villages on the Canada shore, are Amerstburgh, near the entrance to Lake Erie, Sandwich, about three miles below Detroit, and Windsor directly opposite the city. On the American shore, Gibraltei, opposite Amherstburgh, Trenton opposite Grosse Isle, and Wyandotte, about ten miles below the city.

Fort Malden is situated just above the village of Amerstburgh, in Canada and Fort Wayne is situated on the American shore, on the Sand Hill, about three miles below the city

THE CLIMATE.

The climate of Detroit is temperate; snow falls at from six to eighteen inches deep, and never remains more than a few weeks. The transition from the cold of spring to the heat of summer is rapid, from summer to winter gradual and prolonged. As general characteristics, the spring is wet and prolonged; summer dry; autumn mild; winter cold and dry The average temperature in the spring is 50 Farenheit, summer 80; winter 20; autumn 60 to 65

ELEVATIONS.

The elevations of different localities in the city, above the Detroit River is as follows:

Jefferson Avenue from the Michigan Central R R Depot to the east line of the city at the intersection of different sts

Street	ft
At Third street,	4 ft.
" Second "	5
" First "	6
" Cass "	18
" Wayne "	25
" Shelby "	28
" Griswold "	28
" Woodward Ave.	26
" Bates street,	26
" Randolph street,	26
" Brush street,	26
" Beaubien street,	26
" St. Antoine "	27
" Hastings "	29
" Rivard "	31
" Russell "	26
" Riopelle "	23
" Orleans "	20
Lafayette Street.	
At Griswold street,	27
" Shelby "	31
" Wayne "	31
" Cass "	31
" First "	31
" Second "	29
" Third "	30
" Fourth "	29
" Fifth "	29
" Sixth "	28
" Seventh "	26
" Eighth "	25

Fort street from Woodward Avenue to the west line of the city

Street	ft
At Woodward Ave.	23 ft
" Griswold street,	29
" Shelby "	33
" Wayne "	34
" Cass "	33
" First "	33
" Second "	31
" Third "	27
" Fourth "	25
" Fifth "	23
" Sixth "	21
" Seventh "	20
" Eighth "	19

Woodward Avenue from the River to the north line of the city

Street	ft
At Atwater street,	6 ft
" Woodbridge st.	15
" Jefferson Ave,	26
" Larned street,	25
" Congress "	20
" Fort "	23
" State "	26
" Grand River st.,	24
" Clifford street,	23
" Grand Circus st.	25
" Adams Avenue,	28
" Elizabeth street,	28
" Montcalm "	29
" High "	32
" Henry "	35
" Sibley "	37
" Toll Gate,	50
" North line city,	58
Gratiot Road at Orleans st.,	45

The country back of the city gradually rises until it reaches at Birmingham, 18 miles from the city, an elevation of 200 feet above the Detroit River, and Pontiac 25 miles north of the city, is 386 feet above the river, and the Detroit and Milwaukee Rail Road passes over an elevation of 400 feet between Detroit and Pontiac.

FIRES—FIRE DEPARTMENT.

Few cities of its size have suffered by fire to the same extent as the city of Detroit has. In 1704 an attempt was made by the Indians to destroy it by fire who partly succeeded. In 1805 it was almost entirely consumed (but one house escaped.) In 1837 nearly four squares in the business part of the city were destroyed. In 1842 one of the best business squares in the city was entirely swept off, and in 1848 four squares were burnt over in the centre of the city. Besides these several very severe and calamitous fires might be enumerated. The first Fire Engine Company was organized in 1815, and the engine used by this Company was taken from Commodore Perry's Flag Ship—previous to this a "bag, bucket and battering ram comp'y" had been organized, and the inhabitants were required under penalty to keep on their respective premises a certain quantity of water in a wooden cask arranged with handles and provided with a pole so that two men could sling it upon their shoulders and convey it to a fire. Each house was to be provided with a ladder and a certain number of buckets.

The first engine purchased by the city was purchased in 1825 by Hon. J. R. Williams, then Mayor of Detroit, to man which a company was organized and called "Protection Engine Company No. 1." In 1827 another Engine was procured and a Company organized to man the same which was called "Eagle Company No. 2." In 1840 the Fire Department consisted of Four Engine Companies, "Protection No. 1," "Eagle No. 2," "Wolverine No. 3," "LaFayette No. 4," one Hose Company, "Hurlbut No. 1," and one Hook, Ladder and Axe Company.

The Legislature in 1840 granted a charter to the Department—the officers named in the act were Robert L. Roberts, President, Frederick Buhl Vice President, Edmund R. Kearsley, Secretary, Darius Lamson, Treasurer and Elijah Goodell, Collector. The firemen of the city having previously organized the Department and elected the foregoing persons as officers.

Subsequently the following gentlemen have been elected to and discharged the duties of President: John Owen, Chauncy Hurlbut, David Smart, J. A. Van Dyke, Eben N. Wilcox, and John Patton.

Shortly after the organization of the Department an effort was made to raise a fund ostensibly for the benefit of widows and orphans of members of the Department. A small amount was at first realized, but this was carefully fostered and loaned on interest, which, with the amount received from the annual balls, given by the Department, the annual donations from citizens, which were always liberal, the fund in 1849, besides the amount paid for relief, amounted to something over $6,000 with which was purchased a lot, and it was determined to erect thereon a Hall. Proposals were received, and it was ascertained that to erect a suitable building would cost $15,000. The firemen at once determined to erect the building, and authorized the President, Hon. James A. Van Dyke, to effect a loan to the amount of $8,000 secured on the property, which he accomplished, and the building was put under contract, relying upon the liberality of their fellow citizens to aid in completing it, and the promptness with which they came forward to their aid, when it was found that they had gone to the extent of their means, showed that no false estimate was placed on their liberality. The ladies, too, always ready to lend their aid to every good work, came to their rescue, and got up a Fair to increase their fund, from which was realized a little short of $1,000—finding a sufficient remuneration to them for the labor and expense bestowed to witness the completion of an edifice, from which, in all after time, the firemen will derive an annual income, which will enable them to contribute to the widows, and education of the orphans of their members.

The Hall was completed in the fall of 1851, and opened to the public, when Mad'lle Parodi gave her first concert in this city in it, who said of it—" I think it one of the very best that I ever sang in, and the comforable arrangement for the performers is an admirable feature in the building." It is alike the monument of the liberality and gratitude of our citizens, for which they are distinguished, and the prudence and good management of the Department in fostering their means to enable them to erect it.

The amount due on the building will soon be swept away, leaving a permanent and perpetual income of about $2,000 per annum, to be used for benevolent purposes, which result is certainly gratifying to the originators and projectors of the enterprise, as well as to all who have contributed either in labor or means, to accomplish it.

David Smart Esq , is deserving of the gratitude and thanks of every member of the Department, for his untiring efforts in raising the first funds which was the foundation of the noble result. But to the Hon James A. Van Dyke were they particularly indebted for the early erection of the Hall, who (notwithstanding his own multiplied and pressing engagements,) devoted much of his time and energies during the three years he served as President of the Department, for the accomplishment of this object. On the completion of the Hall, Mr. Van Dyke retired from the Presidency, when the Department tendered him its "thanks for his untiring zeal and successful efforts in promoting its good, and resolved, as a token of their high esteem and affectionate regard to procure a full length portrait of him to adorn those walls he had devoted so much time to raise. The portrait, painted by the eminent artist, Hicks, of New York, was procured and elegantly framed, at an expense, in all, of near seven hundred dollars.

The following gentlemen have, in turn, held the office of Chief Engineer of the Department·

Levi Cook, Noah Sutton, Henry V. Dishrow, Theodore Williams, Chauncy Hurlbut, James Stewart, William Barclay, William Duncan, Lucretius H Cobb and John Patton. William Duncan present incumbent.

The Fire Department at present consists of 8 Engines, "Protection No 1," 'Eagle No. 2," "Wolverine No 3," "LaFayette No. 4," "Washington No 5," "Neptune No 6," "Union No. 7," and "Continentals No 8,' and one Hook, Ladder and Axe Company. Each of the several Companies have very substantial brick houses, two stories high, some of whom have very elegantly furnished meeting rooms. That of the "Eagles," it is believed is not excelled by any Fire Company in the United States.

YOUNG MENS' SOCIETY.

The Detroit Young Men's Society was organized in January 1843, when the late Dr. Douglass Houghton delivered the first lecture before the association. On the 26th, of March 1836 the Society was incorporated by the Legislature.

The exercises of the Society are continued only during the fall and winter months, and consist of debates and lectures alternately one evening in every week.

In 1850 the Society purchased a very desirable lot, 48 feet front and 100 feet deep, on Jefferson Avenue, between Bates and Randolph streets, and erected a superb building thereon 48 by 95 feet. On the first floor are two spacious stores, over which is their elegant Hall. The entrance to the Hall is between the two stores, over the entrance and front part of the stores are appropriate committee and library rooms. The Society have a large and well selected Library of about 3000 volumes.

The following gentlemen have been elected to and discharged the duties of President of the Society, as follows :

In 1833, Franklin Sawyer, Jr.,
    Douglass Houghton,
In 1834, Jacob M. Howard,
    Charles W. Penny,
In 1835, George C. Bates,
    Marshall J. Bacon,
    James A. Armstrong,
In 1836, John N. Talbot,
    Alexander W. Buel,
    George E. Hand,
In 1837, David E. Harbaugh,
In 1838, Franklin Sawyer, Jr.,
In 1839, James A. Van Dyke,
In 1840, John G. Atterbury,
In 1841, Samuel Barstow,

In 1842, John S. Abbott,
In 1843, Samuel T. Douglass,
In 1844, Asher S. Kellogg,
In 1845, Bela Hubbard,
In 1846, Witter J. Baxter,
In 1847, Thomas W. Lockwood,
In 1848, James V. Campbell,
In 1849, Ed. C. Walker,
In 1850, D. Bethune Duffield,
In 1851, U. Tracy Howe,
In 1852, Halmer H. Emmons,
In 1853, George V. N. Lothrop,
In 1854, Charles I. Walker,
In 1855, Levi Bishop.

MECHANICS' SOCIETY.

The Mechanics' Society of the City of Detroit, was founded in the year 1818, and incorporated by an act of the Governor and Judges of the Territory of Michigan, in 1820, their charter was renewed in 1839 by the State Legislature.

The Society own a very elligibly situated lot, about one hundred feet square on the corner of Griswold and LaFayette streets on which their Hall is situated. It is in contemplation to erect on this site a large and elegant Hall. They have a well selected Library of about 2000 volumes, and it is the very place where every young mechanic and apprentice can store his mind with all that has been published upon the arts and sciences. Could an arrangement be made with this and the Young Men's Society whereby their Libraries could be united they would together form a Library unequalled in the west, and such an arrangement no doubt would be to the mutual advantage of both Societies.

LAKE NAVIGATION.

Up to 1679 the lakes were only navigated by birch bark canoes. But in August of that year, the first vessel that ever crossed Lake Erie, arrived at Detroit. This vessel was sixty tons burden, and called the 'Griffin' it was constructed at Erie, then Fort Frontinac, by Robert de LaSalle her commander. Father Louis Hennepin, a missionary was among the passengers. The Griffin proceeded up the Lake to Green Bay, from which place she sailed on the 18th, of September, on her return with a cargo of furs, and was lost on Lake Erie, with all on board. Other vessels were afterwards at an early day constructed of a greater burden and in 1793 the British Government had a number of men-of-war on the Lakes, of two hundred tons burden, each carrying eight guns.

September 10th, 1813, the hostile fleets of England and the United States on Lake Erie, met at the head of the Lake, and a very severe battle ensued. The fleet bearing the 'red cross' of England, consisted of six vessels, carrying sixty-four guns, under command of the veteran Commodore Barclay, and the fleet bearing the 'broad stripes and bright stars' of the United States, consisted of nine vessels, carrying fifty-four guns, under command of the young and inexperienced, but brave Commodore Perry. The result of this conflict was made known to the world in the following dispatch, written at 4 P. M., of that day.

DEAR GENERAL.—We have met the enemy, and they are ours. Two ships, two brigs, one schooner and one sloop. With esteem, &c.,

General William Jones   O. H. PERRY.

Captain Chelsea Blake, that veteran sailor, so long and favorably known on these waters as "COMMODORE OF THE LAKES, and who for many years, sailed the splendid steamers Michigan and Illinois, built by his early and steadfast friend, Oliver Newbury, Esq., of this city, commanded the good schooner General Jackson in 1816, then owned by Messrs. Mack & Conant, of this city. For so many years and so intimately—through battle breeze and storm had our citizens known Blake, from the time he volunteered to sustain his country's flag under General Scott, at Lundy's Lane, until through every vicissitude of a sailor's life, he had won for himself the distinguishing title which he bore at his death, that his name must forever be associated with the lake, which became his favorite element. Of almost giant size, and commanding presence, no son of Neptune ever united in his composition a rarer combination of the qualities which make a true seaman, a safe commander, a genuine hero.

Rough as the billows whose impotent assaults on his vessel he ever laughed to scorn, with voice as hoarse as the tempest which he delighted to rule, this gallant son of the sea had withal a woman's tenderness of heart to answer the appeals of distress. Sincere was the grief of many he had relieved, and universal the regret among all who had ever sailed with him, when he fell a victim to cholera, at Milwaukee, in the year 1849.

Scarcely less closely associated with the rise and progress of vessel and steam navigation on the lakes, is the name of our respected fellow citizen, Oliver Newbury, who has also entitled himself to, and received the rank of "ADMIRAL OF THE LAKES." As he still survives his favorite Captain, it may be unbecoming to speak of him in the terms which his persistent enterprise through the lapse of so many long years, justly deserves. From the commencement of his career in this city, to the present time, he has been more or less largely interested as owner of schooners, brigs, ships and steamers, always of the first class in their day, and at one time ranked as the proprietor of the largest fleet on the great chain of lakes. For the good he has done by the employment of so many, and the promotion of the city's name for spirit and enterprise among the proudest cities of the land, his memory will always be cherished with affection and pride.

The General Jackson was subsequently commanded by our venerated townsman still living, Commodore Brevort, and was wrecked a few years after on Lake Huron. Commodore Brevort also bore a gallant part in Perry's conflict, in testimony and grateful recognition of which his country voted him a gold medal.

In 1817 the published marine list chronicled as the arrivals during the week ending July 24th, ten schooners and one sloop, the latter having the passengers on board—and clearances, one sloop, and six schooners. In 1854, the arrival of vessels at this port, during the season, numbered 2,134, their aggregate tonnage was 1,048,194, and the clearances numbered 2,554, aggregate tonnage 1,244,137.

The number of vessels enrolled at the Detroit Custom House in September 1855, is as follows: steam boats, 60, and steam propellers, 23—tonnage 34,285,30-95. *Sail vessels*—barques 5, brigs 9, schooners 123, scow schooners 15, scows 17, sloops 44—total, 213—tonnage, 35,653, 50-95. Total tonnage of steam and sail vessels, 69,878 80-95, making together of steam boats and sail vessels enrolled in this district about three hundred, the largest of which, the steamer "Western World," is 2,002 tons burden.

STEAM BOATS AND STEAM BOAT ROUTES

The Steam Boat Walk-in-the-Water, Captain Jedediah Rogers, was the first Steamer that navigated the lakes, and her arrival at Detroit for the first time, was chronicled May 20th, 1819.

The following notice of a trip to Mackinaw, appeared at that date in a New York City paper:

"The swift Steamboat, Walk-in-the-Water, is intended to make a voyage early in the summer from Buffalo on Lake Erie, to Michilimackinack, on Lake Huron, for the conveyance of company. The trip has so near a resemblance to the famous Argonautic expedition in the heroic ages of Greece, that expectation is quite alive on the subject. Many of our most distinguished citizens are said to have already engaged their passage for this splendid adventure."

The Walk-in-the-Water was advertised to make one trip weekly, from Black Rock to Detroit, and back, touching at the principal towns on the American shore.

The "Walk-in-the-Water was wrecked near Buffalo, in the fall of 1821. Thomas Palmer, Esq., and lady and Mrs Felix Hinchman of this city, were on board at the time, no lives were lost. The Steam Boat Superior was built during the following winter, under the superintendance of Captain Rogers, and was launched in the month of May, 1822, and made tri-monthly trips, from Buffalo to Detroit during the summer.

This was the commencement of the era of steam in navigation—and now in 1855, there are times when there is not room at our two miles of wharves for the number of steamers that throng them—many of which are magnificent, and as perfect specimens of steam craft as can be found in the world, and the broad stream is frequently for miles above and below the city, studded and whitened with the sails of whole fleets of brigs, schooners and sloops.

Steam boats for the conveyance of passengers now leave this city regularly, as follows:

From Detroit to Buffalo, Daily.—Three magnificent steamers, consisting of the "Wes-

SKETCHES OF THE CITY OF DETROIT.   49

tern World," 2,002 tons burden; "Plymouth Rock," 1,991 tons burden; and "Buckeye State," 1,274 tons burden, form a daily line, connecting at Detroit with the M. C. R. R. These boats make the trip on the north shore, and go through without stopping—running time 15 hours.

From Detroit to Port Huron, Daily.—The splendid steamers "Forester" and "Ruby," form a daily line. Through by daylight.

From Detroit to Ports on Lake Superior—Four magnificent steamers, consisting of the "Illinois," "North Star," "Planet," and "Northerner," ply regularly to Ontonagon and other ports on Lake Superior passing through the Sault Ste Mary Canal.

From Detroit to Cleveland, Daily—Steamers "May Queen" and "Ocean."

From Detroit to Sandusky—Steamer "Bay City"—daily.

From Detroit to Toledo, Daily—Steamers "Dart" and "Arrow."

From Detroit to Ashley—Steamers "Albion" and "Pearl."

From Detroit to Port Sarnia, C W.—Steamer "Canadian."

The Steam Boats "Transit," "Mohawk," and "Argo," (ferries) ply constantly between Detroit and Windsor.

Three regular lines of PROPELLERS are established as follows:

From Detroit to Dunkirk, connecting at Dunkirk with the New York & Erie Rail Road.

From Detroit to Buffalo, connecting at Buffalo with the New York Central Rail Road and Erie Canal.

From Detroit to Ogdensburgh and Cape Vincent, Lake Ontario, passing through the Welland Canal, connecting with the Ogdensburgh and Vermont Central Rail Road, between Ogdensburgh and Boston, and Cape Vincent Rail Road, between New York and Cape Vincent.

Besides these a large number of propellers are engaged in carrying freight to various ports on the Lakes, above and below, and thousands of brigs and schooners arrive and clear during a season.

RAIL ROADS.

"The first railways, formed on the plan of making a distinct surface and track for the wheels seems to have been constructed near Newcastle upon the river Tyne in England. In Roger North's Life of Lord Keeper North, he says, that at this place (in 1676) the coals were conveyed from the mines to the banks of the river, by laying rails of timber exactly strait and parallel; and bulky carts were made with four rollers fitting those rails, whereby the carriage was made so easy that one horse would draw four or five chaldrons of coal." In 1776, Mr. Carr constructed an iron railroad at the Sheffield colliery. The rails were supported by wooden sleepers, to which they were nailed. Railways were afterward used in a number of other collieries, and in 1825 the first railway was successfully adopted on a public thoroughfare for the tranportation of merchandise and passengers on the Stockton and Darlington railroad in England, 25 miles in length. From that time a new era commenced in the history of railroad transportation and railroads now extend like a network over the greater part of England. The first locomotive engine used as the motive power on railroads was used on the Liverpool and Manchester Railway in 1830. In 1827 the first railroad in the United States was constructed from Quincy near Boston to Neponset river, a distance of three miles. It was constructed solely for the transportation of granite from the quarries. In 1828 the Mauch Chunck Railroad, nine miles in length, was finished, this was constructed solely for the transportation of coal. In 1826 the Legislature of the State of New York chartered the "Hudson and Mohawk Railroad Company," which was the first railroad company chartered in the United States. On the 12th day of August, 1830, the first ground was broken at Schenectaday for a double track road to Albany, and the road was in operation the following spring. The cars used were coach bod ies, of the ordinary form. The motive power first used was horse, and on steep inclinations stationary steam power. A locomotive engine called "John Bull," procured from England, was placed on it during that year. The Newcastle and Frenchtown Railroad was constructed in 1829. This road extended from Newcastle on the Delaware, to the Elk river, near Frenchtown, 16¼ miles, and was the first railroad constructed in the United States for the conveyance of passengers. The first engine on a railroad weighed but six tons, while at the present day engines of forty tons weight (including tenders) have been introduced on some roads.

In 1830 there were but 41 miles of railroad in operation in the United States, in 1840, 2,167 miles, in 1850, 8,659 miles, and in 1854 there were 430 railroads in operation, having an aggregate length of 20,619 miles—4,000 miles of which are double track roads. And it is estimated that there are about 13,000 miles more of railroads now in various stages of construction.

The project of a railroad across the Peninsula of Michigan, was agitated as early as 1830, at which time the Legislature of the then Territory of Michigan adopted a memorial to the general government in favor of the establishment of a canal or railroad route from Detroit to the mouth of St. Joseph River on Lake Michigan.

In 1832 the Legislature incorporated the "Detroit and St. Joseph Railroad Company." In 1834 Lieut. J. M. Berrien, under authority of the War Department surveyed the route of the road and submitted his report to a convention of the friends of the measure, held in Detroit in December of that year. The Directors and officers of the Company were as follows: Maj. John Biddle, *President*, Charles C. Trowbridge, Oliver Newberry, Shubael Conant, E. A. Brush, Henry Whiting, J. Burdick, H. H. Comstock, Mark Norris and C. N. Omsby, *Directors*, John M. Berrien *Chief Engineer*, A. J. Center, *Assistant Engineer*, and A. H. Adams *Secretary and Treasurer*. The construction of the road was commenced by this company in 1836. Who surveyed the road from Detroit to Jackson and located it to Dexter. This company graded about ten miles of the road in detached parts between Detroit and Ypsilanti. They expended for grading iron cars bridges &c., the sum of $139,702.79. Soon after Michigan was admitted into the Union, the Legislature adopted a grand scheme of internal improvements and effected a loan of five millions of dollars for the purpose of constructing public works—railroads and canals. This had the effect to check individual enterprise, and the Detroit and St. Joseph Railroad Company transferred their interests to the State in the year 1837. The State completed and opened the road to Ypsilanti in 1838, to Ann Arbor in 1839, to Jackson in 1842, and to Kalamazoo in 1843. The State constructed the road with the wood and flat bar superstructure as far as Kalamazoo, 143 miles from Detroit. When in 1846 it was purchased from the State by capitalists, from New York and New England, for the sum of two million of dollars and a charter was granted them by the Legislature incorporating them a company under the style of the Michigan Central Railroad Company.

MICHIGAN CENTRAL RAILROAD.

The design of the State was to make a road across the Peninsula only from Detroit to Lake Michigan. But it was at once apparent to the new owners that, with the great and growing west beyond, the ultimate interest of the stockholders—though perhaps temporarily suffering—would be promoted by the construction of a more permanent work, of large capacity, and its extension through the State of Indiana to Chicago, in Illinois. The charter of the company gave them ample power to extend their road through this State, and the company soon made arrangements with the New Albany and Salem Railroad Company to use their right to build a road from Michigan City to the State line of Illinois, and with the Illinois Central Railroad Company, whereby they were enabled to reach Chicago, which they accomplished in 1852. At Chicago the road connects with nearly 1500 miles of Railway and their extensive Steamboat connections.

The Michigan Central Road also now connects with the Joliet and Northern Indiana road at Lake Station, 35 miles east of Chicago, by which arrangement passengers from St. Louis, can be *set down in New York in about forty-eight hours, and freight can be transported between Detroit and the Mississippi River without breaking bulk on the route.* At Detroit the Michigan Central road connects with the Great Western Railway from Detroit to Niagara through Canada West, and with their own line of magnificent Steamers on Lake Erie, which pass down the north shore of the Lake going through without stopping in 15 hours.

They run four passenger trains through from Detroit to Chicago, daily, and one accommodation train from Detroit to Kalamazoo, 143 miles daily.

The aggregate number of passengers conveyed on the road during the year ending May 31st, 1855, was 503,774, (being 145,838 more than the year previous,) making a daily average of nearly 1700. The aggregate number of tons of freight moved on the road during the same time was 241,825, being an increase over the year previous of 25,265 tons. The earnings of the road for the same time amounted to the sum of $2,215,283, being 635,871 more than the year previous and the expenses of the road were for same time $2,335,627 and $431,683 more than the year previous. The net earnings of the road for same time amounted to the sum of $879,656, being $204,180 more than the previous year.

The annual business of the road has increased in the last six years as follows: in the number of passengers conveyed, from 152,672 to 503,664; in the number of tons of freight moved, from 81,066 to 241,826 tons; in gross earnings, from $691,972 to $2,213,283; and in net earnings, from $390,323 to $879,635. The operating expenses from $301,649 to $1,335,627.

The assets of the company are as follows:

Cost of road including depots,	$10,300,147 03
Stock in Steamboats,	343,880 04
Stock and Bonds in other Roads,	1,399,763 99
Total,	$12,043,791 06

There are 64 Locomotive Engines on the road, 11 of which were constructed in the Company's shops in this city, and 4 by the Detroit Locomotive Works, and the others at eastern manufactories. There are on the road 57 first and 12 second class passengercars 630. 8 wheeled box freight cars; 150, 8 wheeled open cars; 11, 4 wheeled box cars.

Total Passenger Cars 69.

Total Freight Cars 1631.

And 20 gravel dumpers, 70 hand cars, and 60 repair and wood cars.

All the cars of every kind in use on this road were built by the company in their own shops; and the company employ about 1200 men in operating the road and car and engine building.

The population of that section of the State tributary to this road is 216,852; the number of acres of improved land 844,309; and the products of the district in 1854 was as follows: 3,137,875 bushels of wheat, 3,450,946 bushels of corn, 943,330 bushels of grain, 1,078,244 bushels of potatoes, 86,760,889 feet of lumber; there are 298 saw mills and 93 flour mills in the section. The Depot grounds of this company, in Detroit, embrace an area of twenty-two acres of land, all enclosed. They have twenty-six hundred feet of dock front on the river. Along this is their freight depot building, constructed of brick, two stories high, one hundred feet wide and eight hundred feet long. This building can store one hundred thousand barrels of flour. Adjoining this, and fronting on Third street, is their Passenger Depot, three hundred and twenty feet long and seventy feet wide; in one end of which are their ticket office, ladies' room, baggage room, &c., on the first floor, and in the second story are the Superintendents and Treasurers' offices, Engineers' Rooms, Local Superintendent and Cashier offices, and also the general ticket office and duplicate bill department. Below the freight depot there are also two large constructed of brick one hundred and twenty feet long sixty feet wide and seventy-five feet high. Besides these there are within the enclosure an engine-house one hundred and thirty five feet diameter, surmounted with a dome eighty-five feet high, with sixteen apartments for engines, two machine and blacksmith shops, one of which is one hundred and sixty feet long, sixty feet wide and two stories high, in which are twenty three forges, the other is one hundred and eighty feet long and fifty five feet wide, having 31 fires, and both furnished with blast from a fan run by a stationary engine. In the second story are a large number of lathes, planing machines, &c., for working iron.

Adjoining is a large shop for building and repairing cars, one hundred and sixty-nine feet long, fifty-five feet wide, and two stories high. All the machinery of this shop and the machine shops is driven by a large stationary engine, placed in a building between the two. There is also between the two a large smoke stack, thirteen feet square and one hundred and fifty feet high, by means of which all the smoke of the shops is carried off by underground flues. There are also lumber, store and other buildings.

This road is second to none in the west in permanency and solidity, or in its conduct and management. It is the pride of our state and city, and has added much to the permanent business of both.

The officers of the company are as follows:

President—J. W. Forbes, Boston.

Vice President—J. W. Brooks, Detroit.

Directors—J. M Forbes, R. B. Forbes, J. F. Thayer, Geo. B. Upton, Boston; D. D. Williamson, John C. Green, New York; Erastus Corning, Albany; J. W. Brooks, Elon Farnsworth, Detroit.

Treasurer—Isaac Livermore.
Superintendent—Reuben N. Rice, Detroit.
Local Treasurer—C. Tracy Howe.
Local Superintendent—Charles M. Hurd.
Cashier—Geo. W. Gilbert.

Freight Agent—John Hosmer.
Auditor—E. Willard Smith.
Supt. Motive Power—S. P. Newhall.
Supt. Car Work—S. C. Case.

DETROIT AND MILWAUKEE RAILWAY.

The "Detroit and Milwaukie Railway Company" was incorporated by the Legislature of Michigan, in February, 1855, with authority to consolidate the Detroit and Pontiac (incorporated in 1834) and the Oakland and Ottowa (incorporated in 1850) Railroad companies, and the consolidation was consummated on the 21st day of April, A. D. 1855, by which act the property, rights and franchises of the "Detroit and Pontiac" and "Oakland and Ottowa" companies were vested in the "Detroit and Milwaukee Railway Company," and placed under the direction of a Board composed of the following gentlemen:

Henry N. Walker, President, Henry Ledyard, Vice President; N. P. Stewart, H. P. Baldwin, B. Wight, E. A. Brush, E. B. Ward, Detroit; W. M. McConnell, Pontiac, H. P. Yale, Grand Rapids, Directors.

O. C. Trowbridge, Secretary and Treasurer.

R. Higham, Chief Engineer.

Names that are a sufficient guarantee to the public to insure the success of any enterprise they undertake.

The Detroit and Milwaukee Railway is to extend from the city of Detroit to Grand Haven, Lake Michigan, 185 miles, passing through the northern tier of counties of the lower peninsula. They are the richest portions of the state, abounding in lumber, plaster, water-lime, coal, salt springs and other valuable elements of wealth. They are also some of the very best farm lands in the state, and yet the least developed, for want of a railway or other available communication commensurate with their business requirements. This road, which is now partially completed, and its construction along the entire length rapidly prosecuted, will soon supply their great deficiency, and pour their products and that of the valleys of the Shiawassee, the Maple and Grand River into the city of Detroit, which is their natural depot and market, at once giving the road a local traffic equal to that of the most favored road in the western states.

The population of that section of the state tributary to this road in 1854 was 241,164. The number of acres of improved land was 820,004, and the products of the district were as follows: 2,329,389 bushels of wheat, 2,081,695 bushels of corn, 872,881 bushels of grain, 1,-140,418 bushels of potatoes, and 350,000,000 feet of lumber. There were at that time 99 flour mills and 352 saw mills in the district.

At Corunna, in Shiawassee county, the road crosses the Bituminous coal beds, which have now been tested for four years and found to be of the best quality, and which will be extensively opened when the means of transporting the coal to a market is afforded, which the construction of this road will do.

At Grand Rapids the line passes the gypsum beds, which are extensively worked now, and will form a large item of freight on this road, to supply the wheat growing counties contiguous to it.

This road when finished, will be a complete work in itself, extending across the entire State, from the straits which connect Lakes Erie and St. Clair, at the city of Detroit, the commercial capital of the State, to Lake Michigan, and might rely solely upon the resources of the contiguous territory along the line for support, but its position as part of the great Northern trunk line, from Boston, New York and Montreal, to the Mississippi River and finally from thence to the Pacific Ocean, gives it in a measure a national character, and secures a large amount of through traffic between the country west of Lake Michigan and the east. The distance by this road, between New York and Milwaukee, is 106 miles shorter than by any other route.

At Detroit the road forms a connection with the Great Western Railway from Detroit to Niagara Falls through Canada West, and from thence by several different routes to the cities on the sea-board, both in the States and Canada.

At Grand Haven on Lake Michigan a connection is formed by steam ferries across the Lake to Milwaukee, connecting with the five different railroads terminating in that city, extending west to the Mississippi River, to-wit: The "Milwaukee and Mississippi," to Prairie du Chien. the "Milwaukee and La Cross," the "Racine, Kenosha and Beloit," the "Manitowoc and St. Paul's," and the "Milwaukee and Dubuque," or Galena Railroad, and also with roads running north to Lake Superior. The road from Detroit passes through the villages of Royal Oak, Birmingham, Pontiac, Waterford, Rose and Holly, in Oakland county; Fentonville, Linden and Gaines, in Genesee county, Owasso and Corunna, in Shiawassee county, St. Johns, in Clinton county, Lyons, Ionia and Flat River, in Ionia county, Grand Rapids, in Kent county, to Grand Haven in Ottowa county.

At the last session of Congress a bill was introduced to donate public lands for the purpose of constructing a railroad running north connecting with this road at Fentonville, to Saginaw and the Straits of Mackinaw, thence to the Sant St. Mary's and from thence through the mineral regions of Lake Superior to Montreal River. And another to Marquette River in the county of Mason on Lake Michigan, connecting by steamboats across Lake Michigan to Manitowoc, Marquette, Eagle Harbor, and Ontonagon, on Lake Superior. The growing importance of the mining interests on Lake Superior, render a road desirable and its construction will be required at no distant day, which will furnish to the Detroit and Milwaukee road an amount of business not easily appreciated. The Detroit and Milwaukee company received from the Detroit and Pontiac company, twenty-five miles of road from Detroit to Pontiac, which had recently been re-constructed in the best manner, and which was stocked with five locomotives, four passenger cars, and forty-eight freight cars. The road is completed to runna, 50 miles beyond Pontiac, when 75 miles of the road from Detroit will be in operation. Twenty-six hundred tons of iron have recently been received by the company, and the grading and superstructure of the road is rapidly progressing, and the road bed will be ready for the rails as far as Lyons, 123 miles from Detroit, by the first of December next. The estimated cost of the road from Detroit to Lake Michigan is $6,192,050.

The Depot grounds of the company in the city of Detroit are located in the centre of the city on the river, and cover an area of about twelve acres. They have sixteen hundred and fifty feet of dock front on the river. On these grounds there are two large store houses, freight sheds, an engine house for six locomotives, machine shop, smith shop, wood sheds, water tank, &c.

The construction of this road will bring to the city of Detroit an amount of business not easily appreciated and its completion is paramount to every other of the many projected improvements, for the interests and prosperity of the city.

THE GREAT WESTERN RAILWAY.

This popular road, which was opened in January 1854, extends from Windsor, opposite Detroit, through the cities of Chatham, London and Hamilton, to Niagara Falls, 229 miles, crossing the Niagara River on the great Railway Suspension Bridge, acknowledged by all to be one of the wonders of the world, and connecting with the New York Central and New York and Erie Railways, for New York, Boston and all intermediate places. It also connects at Hamilton, with railway and steamers to all ports on Lake Ontario and the River St. Lawrence, and with the Great Western International Line of Steamers for Oswego, which form one of the quickest, and certainly the most pleasant route now open to the East—these steamers being fitted up with every regard to comfort and convenience, and being unsurpassed by any steamers upon the inland waters of America.

The construction of the Great Western Railway, has secured for the city of Detroit what was much needed, and which our citizens have long suffered for the want of, namely, a speedy and reliable route to the east, uninterrupted at all seasons of the year.

The Great Western Railway is acknowledged to be one of the best constructed, and most efficiently managed roads on the continent of America, and has already a very large business, both in through and local traffic, both of which are rapidly increasing.

The receipts for the half year ending 31st

July 1855, being,	£239,193
And for the same period in 1854,	150,105
Showing an increase in one year of	£99,088

or upwards of 66 per cent, on the gross traffic of the line.

There are at present 62 locomotives on the road, and 14 more are to be placed on it this fall, making in all 76. There are likewise on the road 45 first class passenger cars, 29 emigrant cars, 12 baggage, mail and express cars, 416 eight wheel and 100 four wheel box freight cars, 122 platform, 56 cattle and 409 gravel cars; in all 1189, at present on the road, which, with 519 now constructing, will make a total of 1708.

The company have lately issued £1,000,000 of new stock, the whole of which has been taken up by the original shareholders, and they intend at once laying another track between Hamilton and London, to enable them to accommodate their vast and increasing business.

The following are the Directors of the company:

Robt. W. Harris, Esq., President.	William Dickson, Esq.,
John S. Radcliff, Esq., Vice President.	L. B. Smith, Esq.,
C. I. Brydges, Esq., Managing Director.	Alex. Beattie, Esq.,
Henry McKinstry, Esq.,	Robert Gill, Esq.,
Lieut. Col. Gourlay, Esq.	Peter Buchanan, Esq.

Official Directors.—C. Magill, Esq., Mayor of Hamilton; D. Mathieson, Esq., Warden of Oxford; H. Clench, Esq., Warden of Middlesex.

General Office of the Company, Hamilton, Canada West.

THE DETROIT, MONROE AND TOLEDO RAILROAD.

The Detroit, Monroe and Toledo Railroad, which has existed for many years past only in old charters, projected routes and public assurances, is likely to be constructed without further delay. A company was recently organized under the General Railroad Law of Michigan, and the project placed in the hands of a Board of Directors composed of gentlemen of a character that will insure its speedy construction. The Directors have effected such arrangements that will insure the completion of the road within the next twelve months. This road will pass through the villages of Trenton and Wyandot, and Monroe city, to Toledo, connecting us with the southern tier of counties of this State, from which we have hitherto been excluded, and with the Ohio roads, leading to Cincinnati, and the South Shore Rail road to Dunkirk and Buffalo; also, with the Michigan Southern road to Chicago.

The foregoing include all the roads that exist or have a name to do so, but we need others leading to the northern portions of our State. One to Port Huron; one to Saginaw thence to Mackinaw; also one from Detroit to Adrain, thence to the State line to connect with the Logansport and Northern Indiana Railroad, which is already extended to within fifteen miles of our State line, passing through the Wabash and Eel River valleys and connecting with the Mississippi and Atlantic Railroad, forming a direct route to St. Louis, 80 miles less distance from New York than by any other. Let the doors be thrown open wide, and let the citizens of Detroit extend every aid within their power for the construction of roads terminating in the city, wherever they may extend.

DISTANCES FROM DETROIT.

VIA MICHIGAN CENTRAL RAILROAD

	MILES		MILES
To Dearborn	10	To Galesburg	134
Wayne	17	Kalamazoo	143
Ypsilanti	29	Paw Paw	159
Geddes	33	Decatur	167
Ann Arbor	37	Dowagiac	178
Delhi	42	Niles	190
Scio	44	B charan	197
Dexter	48	Terre Coupre	201
Chelsea	54	New Buffalo	217
Grass Lake	65	Porter	229
Jackson	75	Lake	248
Parma	86	Junction	269
Albion	95	Chicago	284
Marshall	107	Joliet	294
Battle Creek	120		

VIA DETROIT AND MILWAUKEE RAILWAY.

To Royal Oak	12	To Corunna	75
Birmingham	16	Owasso	78
Pontiac	26	St. Johns	96
Waterford	31	Lyons	115
Rose	42	Ionia	122
Holly	46	Flat River	137
Fentonville	51	Grand Rapids	155
Linden	55	Grand Haven	184
Gaines	63		

VIA GREAT WESTERN RAILWAY, C. W.

To Belle River	16	To Paris	158
Baptist Creek	30	Fairchild's Creek	167
Chatham	43	Dundas	181
Thamesville	60	Hamilton	186
Hagert's Road	73	Bt ney Creek	193
Eckford	84	Grimsby	203
Loho	100	Beam ville	208
London	110	St. Catharine's	210
Huffman	120	Thorold	221
Ingersoll	129	Niagara Falls	230
Woodstock	138	Batavia	261
Blenheim	147		

VIA PLANKROAD.

To Trenton	15	To Monroe	43
Gibralter	20	Toledo	65

VIA DETROIT, HOWELL AND LANSING PLANKROAD

To Redford	12	To Williamstown	70
Farmington	19	Okemos	77
Novi	25	Lansing	86
Hickville	30	Eagle	91
New Hudson	32	Portland	108
Kensington	34	Lyons	113
Brighton	40	Ionia	117
Howell	50	Saranac (per S B)	132
Fowler's	59	Ada	164
Le Roy	68	Grand Rapids	151

VIA DETROIT AND SALINE PLANKROAD.

To Dearborn	10	To Clinton	52
Wayne	17	Tecumseh	57
Ypsilanti	29	Adrian	67
Saline	40		

VIA DETROIT, MT. CLEMENS AND ALMONT PLANKROAD

To Utica	23	To Romeo	30
Mt. Clement	2	Almont	40
Armada	37		

VIA LAKE.

To Ashley	30	To Goderich, C W	178
Algonac	44	Mackinaw	315
Newport	48	Sault St. Maries	335
St. Clair	56	Ontonagon	645
Port Huron	66	Superior City	730
Lexington	88	Green Bay	495

VIA LAKE.

To Monroe	40	Cleveland	110
Toledo	60	Dunkirk	230
Sandusky	75	Buffalo	285

VIA STEAMBOATS.

To Sandusky City	75	To Ashtabula	213
Huron	85	Conneaut	226
Black River	100	Erie	232
Cleveland	142	Dunkirk	286
Grand River	172	Buffalo	325
To Cincinnati	397	To Cairo	649
Pittsburg	505	Galena	625
R Is'and by Chicago	450	St. Paul	644
St. Louis	552	Milwaukee	360

CONCLUSION.

The city of Detroit is the commercial and manufacturing metropolis of the state of Michigan, which is surrounded by a greater extent of navigable waters than any other state in the Union, its territory being washed by the waters of Lakes Erie, St Clair, Huron, Superior and Michigan; and its agricultural resources are great, its pineries are most extensive, its fisheries are superior, its upper Peninsula abounds in mineral wealth. The copper and iron found there is superior in quality and the quantity inexhaustible. Its coal and gypsum, beds and marble quarries are inferior to none, and its salt springs are excelled only in strength by those of New York, all of which are now being appreciated by our citizens, who are putting forth their efforts to fully develope them, satisfied that every element of wealth is within their reach and that the City of the Straits will maintain a proud and preeminent position among her sister cities of the Lakes and the Union.

Three railroads now terminate here, and the fourth will be added within the next twelve months, connecting us with the southern tier of counties of our state, from which we have hitherto been excluded, and with the Ohio roads leading to Cincinnati and beyond, and the Logansport and St. Louis railroad must inevitably extend itself to this city.

The city contains at present numerous extensive manufactories, a population of 50,000, a vast number of prosperous mechanics, mostly owning their own shops and houses. We have an improved city, a magnificent river, never swollen by flood or shallowed by drouth, with a front of miles for wharfage and anchorage every where. As a harbor it is excelled by few in the world, either in picturesqueness or safety.

The country around and tributary to the city is growing and improving not less rapidly, and the site and location of the town is admirably adapted to commercial and mechanical business of every kind and on a large scale. The Sault Ste Marie canal, just completed, opens up to us a hitherto obstructed prospect, and secures a large and valuable trade with the upper portion of the State. The advantages of this trade to Detroit are apparent.

Detroit in many particulars is, notwithstanding the misapprehensions of some letter writers, the unrivalled City of the Lakes. Its growth has been steady, healthy and natural. Portions of the city which but a few years ago were the very outskirts, ponds formerly existing on the Grand Circus and on the farms at the head of the "River Savoyard" where sportsmen amused themselves hunting duck and plover, are now far within the thickly settled and populated districts. The localities formerly occupied by forts, cantonments, block houses, magazines and navy yards, the potato fields, commons where cattle grazed, and grave yards were, are now compactly covered by long rows of stores and warehouses, manufactories, mechanics' shops, dwellings, and towering church steeples, and a dense, thrifty and enterprising population whose busy hum have so changed the scene that the ancient *habitant* and persons born and reared in the land are scarcely able to recognize it. As the poet might say.

> "On lawn and slope—the red man's late abode
> The steam horse rushes on an I on road
> The people fare and was groceries grown
> With products of w de rea m by commerce made our own,
> Ponds where the sportsman hunted duck and plover
> Now with pastures and parks are covered over
> Green lane through which the *habitant* alone
> Drove his *charette*—to a new use it seems to have grown,
> Paved with cobbles which peep out the shore
> Of his house 's rafts'—by tr de yet docked of yore
> Straits whose clear depths no pirogues eel could reach.
> Now sullen ly for back those sewings's ful screech
> Fresh from the "Back Concession"—what our the
> Illumes Jean Crapeau's honest, wondering eyes—
> To see the terrace where the ramparts found,
> With lofty piles of brick and mortar crowned
> Alas! what reater changes braids the modern place
> Containing now a less contented race,
> The simple virtues of the olden time
> Exchanged for coin—the more almighty dime."

APPENDIX.

DETROIT IN 1756.

James Bell, Esq., of this city, has in his possession a bound volume of the "London Chronicle," published in 1757, (The form of the "Chronicle" is 7 by 10 inches, published semi-weekly,) which contains the following:—

"PHILADELPHIA, July 28.

Since our last, came to Town one Peter Lowney, who, for about a year past has been among the French and Indians at Fort Detroit, and informs us as follows, viz: That he was an Ensign of a Company of Rangers in the back part of Virginia, consisting of 70 men, commanded by Capt. John Smith. That last summer the Frontier Inhabitants, being greatly distressed by the incursions of the enemy, their whole company went out in different parties to their assistance, except the Captain himself and nine private men, who were in a Block House and had with them six women and five children.

That on the 30th of June 1756, they were attacked by a body of Indians and some French and defended themselves the best part of a day, in which time, he says, they killed thirty-two Indians and three Frenchmen, lost two of their own people, and another man and himself were wounded; but were forced to surrender at last, the house they were in being set on fire.

That they were then carried off, and after traveling some time, the Indians belonging to four different tribes divided the prisoners, and parted; that before they came to the lower Shawanese Town, (where he supposes there were about 300 Indians) the Shawanese made a sacrifice of one Cole, whom they roasted alive, and tormented for a whole night before he expired; and this they did in sight of the French, who seemed unconcerned at their horrid barbarity, and did not endeavor to restrain them, notwithstanding the moving entreaties and bitter complaints of the poor man; that they also killed and scalped another man on the road, he being old and not able to travel. That he (Lowney) was the only one that was carried to Detroit where there were about 300 French families settled, and in what they call the Town they have about 100 houses; that they have plenty of fish; the land rich, on which they raise wheat and peas, and have very good crops, and the Indians, of two or three different nations very numerous.

That while he was at Detroit an Indian King adopted him for his brother, on which account he was very well used, and was often with them at their Councils with the French, being dressed and painted as the Indians were, and not known by the French but as an Indian, living in every respect as they did; and that at one time in particular, at a conference, he heard the French commander order the Indians to go first to Fort Duquesne, then to Fort Cumberland, and afterwards to destroy all the English inhabitants, that about the beginning of April last a great body of Indians set off for Duquesne, in parties, each party having some Frenchman with them.

That about the middle of June he left Detroit in company with a small party of Indians who were going to Niagara with some furs, in order to purchase Indian goods; that from Detroit to Niagara it is about 280 miles, and that on the Falls of the latter the French have a small Fort, in which they keep 30 men; and at Niagara there is a Fort of 24 guns, 6, 9 and 12 pounders, and in it about 300 men.

That while he was at Niagara he met one William Phillips, of New York, who was taken at Oswego, and they agreed to make their escape together; that the night before they left it, 280 French arrived there from Cadaravui, destined, it was said, for Fort Duquesne, who encamped that night, and were to set out again next day, but he and Phillips went off before them; that they traveled about 200 miles, (the land bad and mostly drowned) when they came to Oswego without seeing an Indian, which place and Fort Ontario they found entirely destroyed; that they came to the Mohawk River, where they were kindly received by the Indians, who gave them some victuals, of which they were in great want; and that they got to Albany the 12th inst., from whence he proceeded to this city, and is now gone to Virginia, where his parents live. He was born in this Town, and is about 23 years of age. Capt. Smith, he said, was given to the French, and sent to Canada in the spring"

DETROIT IN 1766-8.

The compiler of the foregoing Sketches is indebted to Hon. A. D Fraser for the following papers, received after the foregoing were in type. In a note accompanying the papers Mr. Fraser says: "Little is known of the early history of our city; and those who could have shed light upon it have long since passed away. Much, however, might be done in our day towards this object, by the publication of such ancient documents as must be still in the possession of some families in this ancient city. I am led to make these remarks from having recently become possessed of two original documents, which I cannot but think will be perused with some curiosity. They were recently discovered among the papers of a gentleman who died on the opposite shore some forty years ago. It seems that the British Government, about four years after taking possession of Detroit, formed the determination to compel the inhabitants to bear the expense of repairing the Fort at their own cost. Col. John Campble, the commandant at Detroit and its dependencies, issued a requisition on the citizens for this purpose. This drew from them a spirited and energetic remonstrance. The second document is a voluntary association entered into in 1768 by some of the principal inhabitants, to repair the pickets around the Town, as well for the public good, as their own particular and common safety, and appointing commissioners to do the work at their expense."

To JOHN CAMPBLE, ESQ., LIEUT. COL. AND COMMANDANT AT DETROIT AND ITS DEPENDENCIES:—

SIR:—
We have taken your order of the 3d instant, respecting the furnishing of materials by us for repairing this Fort, into consideration, and find it absolutely impossible to comply with it. The requisition made of us per individuals, would amount at least to

ment, and all the trading people from different places now residing here, to pay. However, that we may not be looked upon to be actuated by a spirit of opposition we have taken all the pains in our power to obtain the fullest information we could in regard to the obligation we are supposed to lay under for keeping up the repairs of this Fort upon its present plan. We find, sir, that till the year 1750 the Fort was about half the extent it now is. The inhabitants till then were obliged to furnish one picket for each foot of ground they possessed in front within the Fort, and pay annually two sol per foot to the Crown, by way of quit rent. It was with difficulty that the circumstance of this place could accomplish the payment of their dues to the French King, of which he proved his sensibility by easing the inhabitants of the heavy burthen of furnishing pickets, for from that time the Fort was enlarged upon an entire new plan, at the sole expense of the Crown. This measure was not only necessary for easing the inhabitants but for conveniency of public buildings. The annual tax of two sol per foot in front, was continued till the surrender of this country to the English, since which the service has required such taxes of us that they have been almost unsupportable,—permit us, sir, to mention them and you will see that we stand in greater need of assistance than be obliged to pay any new demands. Capt. Campbell, the first English commandant at Detroit, on his arrival here, levied a tax on the proprietors in the Fort for lodging the troops, which amounted to a very considerable sum, besides each of the farmers were obliged to pay a cord of wood per acre in front. The second year the proprietors paid again for quartering the troops and the farmers furnished double the quantity of wood they did the year before. The third year Col. Gladwin continued the same taxes. The following year, being 1762, the tax within the Fort alone amounted to one hundred and eighty-four pounds, thirteen shillings and four pence. In the year 1764 the taxes came to one hundred and fifty-eight pounds, New York Currency. In the year 1765 you was pleased to signify by Messrs. Babee and Shapperton that the taxes for the future should be the same as in the French Government, which, as we have said before, was two sol per foot for the lots within the Fort. The farmers were subject to a quit rent of two shillings and eight pence, New York Currency, and one-fourth bushel wheat per acre in front, which was accordingly paid to Mr. Shapperton, who was appointed to receive the same. After this, we could not help being surprised at the tax for the current year, viz: one shilling per foot in front for lots within the Fort, and ten shillings per acre for the farmers in the country. The heaviness of this tax is most severely felt, as you may judge by the delay and the difficulty the people have in paying it. This proves the badness of our circumstances. We have not mentioned anything here with a view of throwing any odium on you or any of your predecessors in the command, but to show the impossibility of complying with the requisition now under consideration. To make our plea of exemption still stronger, we take the liberty to lay before you Mr. Navarre's letter to us with its translation, as he has long resided here in a public character, and being a man of knowledge, we cannot doubt but the testimony will have its deserved effect with his Excellency the General. We forbear any further arguments of our inabilities. You know, sir, the sorrowful situation we are reduced to for want of money, and the languishing condition our trade is in. In short, the knowledge you have of everything that relates to this infant country and the countenance and protection you have always showed to a fair trade, makes us hope that you will do us the justice to represent our circumstances as they really are to those in power, and then we are sure we shall be relieved from some of our present embarrassments, instead of being loaded with new taxes. As you are soon to leave this country, it gives us sensible concern that any of your orders should meet with opposition from us, especially when we consider that all your orders preceding this relative to the settlement have ever been founded on the most just and equitable principles. We therefore take this opportunity (as it probably will be the last,) to thank you with hearts full of gratitude for your wise, steady, benevolent and impartial conduct during your command over us. Accept of our sincere and best wishes for your health happiness and prosperity

We are sir, with respect, your most obedient, humble servants."

Power of Proprietors to the Commissioners for repairing the Pickets about the Town of Detroit

Be it known by these presents, that we, the subscribers, proprietors of the Town of Detroit, sensible of the absolute necessity there is at present for repairing the Pickets around the Town, as well for the public good as our own particular and common safety, we do hereby fully authorize and impower Messrs Baby, St Casm, Sterling and Thom Williams, Commissioners for us and in our behalf and stead to buy Pickets and cause them to be planted, and to make such repairs as to them shall seem expedient, and to appoint a person they may approve of, to superintend the carrying on the work, who is to be paid as they may agree. We hereby ratify, confirm and agree to whatsoever they shall do or cause to be done in and about the premises, and engage to pay on demand our respective proportions of the expenses arising therefrom according to our possessions, as we have been lately taxed for the repairs already made

DETROIT, February 24th, 1768

Signed by John Hay, P Dequindre for Steadman, Rinkin & Eagen, D Baby, W V Schaach & Co, Legrand, Ben James for Firrell & Abbott, John Magill, Peter Raven, D Br hm, St. Martin for Ed Pollard, Alex Macomb, B Chipoton, Chociel, John Robinson, Hugh Boyt Jacob, Lansingin Comin Laferte, B Gracke Narlo Mocaut, Teofille Senchagrin, P St. Cosme, Guilbean, Cabajig, Labrosse, Augustin La Foy, Rosume.

1778.

Letter from General Gage to Capt Stephenson 2d Battalion 60th Regiment, Detroit — Preserved among the papers of the late Judge May. No. 20

NEW YORK, April 8th, 1778

SIR Your letters of the 14th and 18th December, are very full on the subject of grants and lands at the Detroit. I am to explain to you that the King has not invested any persons whatever, with the power of granting lands in America, except to his Governors, within the limits of their respective Provinces, and under certain forms and restrictions, and where any purchase is made of the Indians though within the limits of the Province they are not valid, unless permission is given so to do, and the purchase made in presence of the Governor and His Majesty's Superintendent of Indian Affairs From hence you will know that the power of granting lands at the Detroit, remains solely in the King, and that no purchase can be made of Indians but with the king's permission and authority — It may be needless after the above explanation to inform you that all grants made by Lieut. Col Gladwin, Major Bruce or any other British Commander, are null and void and of no value

As for the French grants in general, unless approved of by the Governor General of Canada and registered accordingly, they were not valid; but as for Mons Belestre's grants in the year 1770, they cannot be deemed any other than fraudulent and are by no means to be looked upon as valid, and as for the Indian purchase they were not allowed by the French, nor are they allowed by the English Government, but under the restrictions I have already mentioned.

Monsieur Navarrie's declaration, or certificate may be in part true, but it is not the whole truth. The first settlers with Mons. Sabrevois, were not, perhaps, enjoined to the conditions, imposed afterwards respecting their titles; the Government was glad to get any people to begin the settlement But Mons. Navarrie's conclusion is vague and ill founded. I am well informed in these matters, was three years in possession of the books wherein the files were registered, and received information upon them, the very time in which Mons Belestre's grants were made, which sufficiently points out their being invalid, and that they could not be registered when the government of Canada was on the point of surrendering to the King, and the Capital possessed by his troops. so early as Sept. 1859. Mons. Belestre was not ignorant of these circumstances, and his grants are fraudulent. I am to require of you as soon as this is received, to annul and make void by public act. every concession made by Mons. Belestre in the year 1760 every grant made by any British Commander, without exception, and all Indian purchases whatever, or Indian deeds, not obtained by the King's permission, and authority; and that you do not suffer any settlements to be made with the above titles, or any new settlements to be begun on any pretence whatever, and that you pull down as fast as any persons shall presume to build up, and that you do seize and send down the country all persons who shall be endeavoring to settle among the savages.

I imagine the Indians will be set upon to talk to you on these subjects; you will answer them that the King is tender of their property, and has made regulations to prevent their being cheated, and defrauded; that His Majesty has been induced to make these rules, upon the frequent complaints of the Indian against the white people who have defrauded them of their lands by making a few of them drunk and getting them in that condition to give away their country, to the great disgust of the rest of the nations, and that by such means the Indians have represented that white people have taken great part of their hunting grounds. This has happened to many Indian nations, and unless you stop it in the beginning at the Detroit, the same thing will happen there.

Mr. Grant has engaged to build two vessels for the King, in which business you will please to assist him, and give him such helps as your Garrison affords, whenever he shall demand it. As for the merchants they may build what vessels they please, but you will not suffer either Mr Grant's artificers or sailors to be taken from him. You have acted very properly in that respect already. I understand there is very good cedar to be had which Mr. Grant will now use for the King's vessels, and if you find it necessary, you will reserve the cedar and suffer no persons to cut it, but when it is to be used in the King's service.

I hope that you received the order about fitting out the old vessels for this year's service.

You must continue to take every precaution against accidents from fire, if Mr. Babies stable is so near the magazine as you represent, it must be deemed a nuisance and removed accordingly.

I am sir, your most obedient, humble servant,

(Signed)   THOMAS GAGE.

P. S.—The merchants alledge that there is cedar to be had in the greatest plenty. If that is the real case, I can have no objection to their cutting as much as they shall want of it; and you will not obstruct them, in that or any other business not detrimental to the service.   T. G.

(A true copy.)   E. B. LITTLEHALES.

To Capt. STEPHENSON, 2d Bat. 60th Reg., at Detroit.

1799.

The following extracts are from a letter written by the late Peter Andrain, Esq., father of Mrs. Robert Abbot, to Hon. James May, who was at the time at Cincinnati, then the seat of Government. The letter is dated Detroit, January 14th 1799, and gives in detail the proceedings of an election being held for the election of two members of General Assembly, Judge May being a candidate for re-election. The voting was *viva voce*, and the Judges of election refused to receive votes for Judge May, "because he was gone to Cincinnati." This was the only poll held in Michigan, and the inhabitants, from River Raisin to River St. Clair, came here to vote. The election was held two days and the "candidates proclaimed to be highest in number are Wisewell and Visger, as Col. Chabert has declined, and is not eligible, not having three years' residence in the country. Visger and Wisewell were there present, and Visger told the Judges and Sheriff that he would not go with Wisewell. He then asked them which candidate was the highest in number of votes. They answered him that it was Col. Chabert. Visger said he was willing to go with Col. Chabert. Col. Chabert they then sent for, who was in an adjoining room, and asked him whether he was willing to go with Mr. Visger. He answered yes. Col. Chabert demanded then a certificate of his election, and they answered him that they could not give it. They called for wine, and thus the business ended. Previous to that, Christian Clemens, a friend of Wisewell, asked the Sheriff and Judges why the name of Wisewell was left behind, being reported to be equal, in number of votes, to Visger. The answer was, that 'Visger is an older resident than Wisewell.'"

"THURSDAY, 17TH.

The old, virtuous Col. McKee died at his seat on the river Thames, the day before yesterday, after a short illness. His remains have been interred this afternoon with great pomp at the seat of his son Tom, at Petitte Cota. All the British Grandees attended, even Col. Maisonville. This event will probably damp the rejoicings of to-morrow evening, being the Queen's birth. A grand *bal para* is to be at Mr. Roe's, over the river, and the brave Tom was one of the managers, with Jacques Baby. You must announce to the world, through the medium of the Cincinnati Gazette, this memorable death. Great Britain have lost a great support — the Indians a tender parent, and the United States the most inveterate and unnatural enemy."

"The Captains of the militia on the British side were ordered to furnish five men per each company to go immediately to Malden, to help to picket and fortify that garrison. People seem a little alarmed on that side, and so are our own at the order of the Col. Commandant which was published last Sunday at church, by Mr. Levadoux himself, that the burying ground lately allowed to Roman Catholics should not be picketted, but only defended by a flying fence, &c. Capt Sedgwick told me this morning that orders are received to have this town picketted anew, estimate of that expense is preparing, and it will amount to a pretty penny."

Your mill* has been going a spell, the water wheel got broke and was immediately repaired by Munish Labadi. Messrs Fillio & Memsh have chosen some bolting cloth at Mr McIntosh's, and the bolt is made and at work. Every attention is paid to your interest. No news yet from Wittmore Knaggs—Hamtramck not yet arrived.

FRIDAY, 18TH.

This day the British are celebrating in the house of Mr. Roe, the Queen's birth-day. I can hear the noise of the drum, as the wind blows from that shore. All our officers except Col. Strong, Lukens, Tallman and Gray are there. Ernest and his wife, the Sheriff and his wife, Mrs. and Miss Dodemead and Miss Sally Williams are there, and also James Henry and Winston.

SATURDAY, 19TH.

Your Lady told me this morning that the dam of your mill was damaged near the trunk through which water is conveyed to the wheel.

---

*This was probably the first water flour mill in the State, and the one erected at Pontiac by Messrs Mack and Sibley the first one in the interior.

1812

Copy of an address which was drawn up by Judge May, and signed by the inhabitants residing at Detroit and vicinity, and presented to His Honor, Judge Woodward

To the Honorable Augustus B. Woodward, one of the Judges of the Territory of Michigan

SIR:—We, the inhabitants residing in the vicinity of Detroit, beg leave to state That we have learned with extreme regret, that in consequence of not receiving any answer to your despatches which had been forwarded to the General Government, (after waiting a reasonable time) you have signified your intention of shaping your course in a few days for the city of Washington.

We are on this occasion particularly obliged to acknowledge and admire your patriotic and uniform conduct, since the surrender (on the 16th August last,) of this Territory to His Majesty's arms, in interceding and protecting us suffering citizens and saving our lives and persons from the victorious and insulting savage, in preserving the remnants of our property from pillage, and in aiding the means of departing those who wished to go and find the standard of their country, and also for the spirit of humanity which you have displayed towards the surviving citizens of the unhappy and terrible disaster which took place on the 15th of August last in the vicinity of Chicago*—in procuring the means of preserving those unhappy survivors, from the distressing calamities which environed them, and for their restoration to their friends. We have seen with great satisfaction the good effects which has resulted from your respected efforts, and we sincerely hope that the pains and interest you have taken in our behalf, may be crowned with success.

From the just sense we entertain of your goodness, we cannot reconcile it to our minds that you have any, the least wish or intention to emulate the example of others, who at the hour of danger and at a time their services was most undoubtedly required, immediately abandoned their posts and flew to the United States, leaving us to our fate, and owing entirely to the pains and exertions which you have taken on the occasion, we have happily escaped. Fully impressed from the situation of the country, of the necessity of your presence, the fond hope we entertain that ere long your despatches will be answered and your conduct highly approved by the General Government, we take the liberty of soliciting as a particular favor, that you will continue to remain and brave out the storm with us, or until the General Government shall judge proper to recall you from the Territory. We further beg leave, with the deepest sense of gratitude, for the past exertions which you have manifested in our behalf and for the tranquility which we continue to enjoy, to offer you our warmest thanks.

DETROIT, 6th January, 1813.

---

* The Massacre, by the Pottawotamie Indians, of thirty eight men, two women and twelve children, who that day had left and abandoned Fort Dearborn, and taken up their line of march for Fort Wayne under an escort of Pottawotamie Indians, who after promising to escort them to Fort Wayne and receiving presents of all the Government property in the Fort, proved treacherous and attacked the party within a mile and a half of the Fort, killing about two thirds of the party, when the remainder surrendered. The prisoners were divided among the different bands of Indians, who in time reached Detroit. The commandant, Capt. Heald, and wife, were wounded, as also were Lieut. and Mrs. Helm.

TABLE OF CONTENTS.

	PAGE
The City—its History	3
Detroit in 1778—Interesting Narrative	6
Detroit in 1805—Before the Fire	8
The New Town	8
Time's Changes	9
Mayors	12
Population	13
Property Valuation	13
Public disbursements 1853-4	14
Libraries	14
Hotels	15
Architecture	15
Public Grounds	16
Width of Avenues	17
Mercantile	17
Commerce in 1854	19
Manufactories	20
Lumber	20
Wyandotte	21
The Fish Trade of the Lakes	21
Lake Superior Trade	22
Lake Superior Copper	23
Mining	24
Produce of Copper	25
Lake Superior Iron	26
Lake Superior Marble	28
Coal	28
Salt	30
City Statistics, 1855	30
Schools—Their Early History	31
Common Schools	33

	PAGE
Churches and Religious Societies	4
Cemeteries	36
Water Works	37
New Reservoir	39
Comparative Purity of Water	41
Head of Water	42
Gas Light	42
Pavements and Sewers	43
Plank Roads	43
The River	43
The Climate	44
Elevations	44
Fires—The Fire Department	44
Young Men's Society	46
Mechanics Society	47
Lake Navigation	47
Steamboats and Steamboat Routes	48
Railroads	49
Michigan Central Railroad	50
Detroit and Milwaukee Railway	52
Great Western Railway	54
Detroit, Monroe and Toledo Railroad	55
Distances from Detroit	55
Conclusion	56
APPENDIX	
Detroit in 1756	57
" 1766-8	58
Letter from Gen. Gage, 1778	60
" Peter Audrain 1799	62
Address to Judge Woodward, 1812	63

CPSIA information can be obtained
at www.ICGtesting.com
Printed in the USA
LVHW111950230122
709154LV00008B/1049